To Ruth

and the family we're blessed to love—

Anne, Dean, Allie, and Chris

Noelle, Grace, Jonathan, Lynden, and Catherine

"Pardon me, my lord," Gideon replied,
"but if the Lord *is with us,*
why has all this happened to us?"

Judges 6:13

"*God Is Still for You* is a tall, cool drink of refreshing encouragement for a parched world. Filled with winsome wit and grounded in timely truth, this book offers what we all need: a soul-quenching, living-water kind of hope. So start reading. Get this in the hands of a friend. You'll be glad you did."

—Geof Morin, president and CEO of Biblica

"Bob Page is the real deal. His story will help you see just how absolutely crazy in love God is with you (yes, you!) and how God is always in your corner, even when you feel the most alone. In fact, especially when you feel the most alone."

—Kent Whitaker, *New York Times* best-selling author of *Murder by Family*

"Chaplain Bob Page is widely recognized as godfather to a generation of Air Force chaplains who wanted to be just like him. I certainly did! The humblest general officer I have ever known, he's also the best storyteller I have ever heard. This page-turner will keep you on the edge of your seat as he walks you through the trenches of discouragement and disappointment, conflict and combat, fear and faith, heartache and hope."

—Dondi E. Costin, PhD, chaplain, retired major general of the US Air Force, and president of Liberty University

"In a world where challenges are never in short supply, Chaplain Bob Page delivers a timely reminder that God has never—and will never—abandon us. As a practitioner shaped by a lifetime of service both in and out of uniform, Chaplain Page gently guides us back to the unwavering truth of God's love and presence. This book is more than a message—it's a ministry of hope, healing, spiritual strength, and a call to serve others."

—JoAnne "Jo" Bass, 19th chief master sergeant of the Air Force

"Bob has been a true friend to me, especially when I was in a dark period of my life. The light of hope I saw then came shining through again, ever so brightly, while I read each chapter of *God Is Still for You*. I pray the same thing happens for you!"

—Ronnie D. Hawkins Jr., retired lieutenant general of the US Air Force and president of Angelo State University

"Chaplain Page is able to weave the Lord's truth into all situations, from unexpected events, to answers we didn't want, to times of silence when we don't hear from God at all. Chaplain Page brings understanding and comfort from his civilian, ministerial, and military life experiences."

—Jason Brown, president and CEO of Marketplace Chaplains

"This is the right topic for our troubled times. Bob Page, a friend of Marketplace Chaplains, has the antidote for despair, depression, and discouragement—hope! Here's the perfect book to put into the hands of a friend or loved one who is feeling downcast and heartbroken. I have the highest regard for Bob Page, a devout Christian gentleman and a true patriot."

—Robin Lewis, governing board chair of Marketplace Chaplains

"If you've ever struggled when life doesn't turn out the way you expected, this book will flood you with hope and a sense of how much you matter to God. Dr. Page tells gripping stories peppered with quips that will make you smile and help you see possibility even when your heart is broken."

—Sarah White, executive director of Second Mile Mission Center

GOD IS STILL FOR YOU

Ten Reasons You Can Be Sure Even When Life Is Hard

BOB PAGE

FOREWORD BY DR. DONDI E. COSTIN

God Is Still for You: Ten Reasons You Can Be Sure Even When Life Is Hard

Published by Kregel Publications, a division of Kregel Inc., 2450 Oak Industrial Dr. NE, Grand Rapids, MI 49505. www.kregel.com.

Published in association with the literary agency of Credo Communications, LLC, Grand Rapids, Michigan, www.credocommunications.net.

A portion of the author's profits will support the work of Marketplace Chaplains in caring for employees and their families.

The persons and events portrayed in this book have been used with permission. To protect the privacy of these individuals, some names and identifying details have been changed.

Italics in Scripture indicate the author's added emphasis.

Cataloging-in-Publication Data is available from the Library of Congress.

ISBN 978-0-8254-4990-1, print
ISBN 978-0-8254-4992-5, epub
ISBN 978-0-8254-4991-8, Kindle

Printed in the United States of America
25 26 27 28 29 30 31 32 33 34 / 5 4 3 2 1

CONTENTS

Foreword by Dr. Dondi E. Costin 9

Preface 13

Introduction: Hope in the Desert. 15

Chapter 1: The God Who Never Sleeps. 20

Chapter 2: Roadblocks and Detours 34

Chapter 3: A Brass Coin and Solid-Gold Truth 51

Chapter 4: Night Vision Goggles 68

Chapter 5: All Us Sparrows 82

Chapter 6: Outliers and Outcasts 97

Chapter 7: Hope like Water 111

Chapter 8: Jesus, Job, and Bubba 125

Chapter 9: Your New Best Friend 138

Chapter 10: This Changes Everything 151

Chapter 11: Your Best Life 169

Ten Reasons You Can Be Sure God Is Still for You . . 185

Acknowledgments 187

Notes 189

About the Author. 195

FOREWORD

Like it or not, suffering is the common thread running through the fabric of human history. Long before calendars were created and clocks told time, people in every culture and on every continent were pummeled by the problem of pain. It's our turn now.

Despite our best efforts to wish it away, pain is the one reality we all share, the one problem no formula can fix, and the one prompt that almost always leads to this unanswerable question: "Why me?"

For a host of reasons familiar to both sufferer and philosopher alike, attempts to solve this riddle usually come up dry. Because no answer to that perplexing question will ever truly satisfy, we're better off asking a different question: "Now what?"

Since nobody is exempt from the problem of pain, trying to trace the source of your suffering is as frustrating as it is fruitless. Jesus told us that the sun rises on the evil and the good, just as rain falls on the righteous and the unrighteous (Matthew 5:45). He made it clear that "in this world you will have trouble," which is strangely comforting because it softens the shock when trouble comes. Thankfully, that minor comfort is magnified as Jesus finished with a flourish: "But take heart! I have overcome the world" (John 16:33).

Regardless of where you find yourself or how you got there, this masterful book is a page-turning reminder that God is still for you. He always was and always will be, even when your circumstances tempt you to believe otherwise. Exploding from the heart of Dr. Bob Page, a fellow traveler with a lifetime of helping others to mine meaning from their painful paths, *God Is Still for You* unveils the vital truth of the matter by revealing the heart of God, who "will never leave you nor forsake you" (Hebrews 13:5 ESV).

Dr. Page has mentored me for decades. Because of my respect for his rank and undying gratitude for his impact on me, I have never called him by his first name despite his protests. His formal titles are many: reverend, doctor, chaplain, general. To those I would add servant, leader, pastor, and sage. To me, though, this man of God will forever be Chaplain Page. As you read this life-changing book, my prayer is that you will allow him to become the same for you. The more you do so, the more you will realize that God is still for you.

Having invested the bulk of my career in the business of life transformation—first as a chaplain, then as an educator—I am increasingly convinced of the wisdom captured in this fundamental principle: "When the student is ready, the teacher will appear." This ancient proverb foreshadows what modern educational theorists call *learner readiness*, the idea that students learn best when they are hungry to learn.

When pain pounces, we either descend into despair or grow stronger through suffering. The perspective we choose—"Why me?" or "Now what?"—makes all the difference. Like most trials by fire, the vehicles God uses to build our characters usually differ from what we would choose if we were allowed to pick our own poisons. Even if "no pain, no gain" is the real deal, we don't have to like it. But the perspective we harness in hardship is a choice only we can make—a choice only *you* can make. Pain can be either your prosecutor or your professor. It can either break you or make you. You decide.

Sometimes you don't know what you don't know until circumstances make you wish you had known more ahead of time. Other times you discover that your real need is not learning a new thing but being reminded of an old thing. Yet when you finally get around to filling the knowledge gap, the longed-for "Aha!" moment turns the tide.

If that's what you're seeking, then this book is exactly what you need.

It's been said that every person on the planet is either smack-dab in the middle of trouble, just coming out of it, or about to go in. If trouble has you on the ropes, don't throw in the towel. The teacher is ready when you are. I have learned loads from Chaplain Page over the years, and in this book he'll show you how to make pain your professor, and he'll take you to the head of the class. He'll help you let go of "Why me?" and embrace a life of "Now what?"

God loves you more than you could possibly know. He is still for you. This book will help you experience those truths like never before.

Dondi E. Costin, PhD
Retired Major General, US Air Force
President of Liberty University
Lynchburg, Virginia

PREFACE

Life can change in one totally unexpected moment. A diagnosis. A betrayal. A layoff. A phone call with news you can hardly believe is true. Suddenly the ground gives way beneath you, and you wonder, *Where is God?* In your pain you cry out, "Have you abandoned me?" Fear, like a lead weight, pulls you into the depths, and you hear the Enemy whisper three terrifying words: "You are alone."

Maybe you or someone you love is suffering through a double tragedy like this: You're suffering a wound from some unwanted circumstance that has invaded your life, and your pain is made greater because your faith has been shaken. You imagine God is against you, or you wonder whether he is even there. You are twice wounded.

You continue to show up for work. You may even go through the motions of a faith in God that once burned brightly, but inwardly you're not sure what you believe about God—or yourself—anymore. I wish we could chat. In the absence of a face-to-face, heart-to-heart talk, would you let this book be my side of a conversation with you? If you'll do that, I'd like to come alongside you with the truth that God is for you despite what your circumstances may lead you to believe. If I could sit with you and listen to your story without judgment, as chaplains do, my prayer would be that somewhere along the way in our conversation, God would open your eyes to see his undiminished love for you and the path to hope that his grace always provides.

Introduction

HOPE IN THE DESERT

How in the world did I get here? Ever ask yourself that question? I have, and I remember the time and place. I was standing at the window of my fourth-floor E Ring Pentagon office.[1] I was gazing out across acres of parked cars at the three stainless-steel spires of the Air Force Memorial soaring 270 feet into a cloudless azure sky overlooking Arlington National Cemetery. My journey to this window was an unexpected one. My wife and I had been making plans to retire from the Air Force in San Antonio, Texas, when I got the news that President Barack Obama had nominated me for promotion to brigadier general. Several months later, the Senate confirmed my nomination.

I was an unlikely candidate, to be sure. While I had a strong military record with the prerequisite Major Command assignments, there were some significant holes. I'd never been selected to attend Professional Military Education (PME) in residence. All my PME was completed as distance learning. I was not an Air Force Academy graduate, and I'd never had an Academy assignment. These are things you'd typically find in a general officer's record. Oh, and I didn't play golf. Okay, I added that last one for fun, but you get the point.

Just the numbers made it improbable. Only about 2 percent of Air Force officers are promoted to colonel. On top of that, only one chaplain colonel is promoted to brigadier general every three or four years. As a colonel, chances are you'll be considered for promotion to one star no more than twice in your career. In 2012, out of thirty-four chaplain colonels in the Air Force, only one would be chosen for promotion. Somehow in God's providence, I was selected.

For me, the road to brigadier general was a long and winding one. As it turned out, it was a bit too long and winding. Three years later, it came time to select the next two-star chief of chaplains, and at sixty-three years of age, I had run out of airspeed. The law required brigadier and major generals to retire no later than the first day of the first month after their sixty-fourth birthdays. I retired January 1, 2016, thankful for the thirty-three years God allowed me to be an airman. I was grateful for the people we'd come to love like family, for the places we'd been, and for the rare view of the world from the E Ring I was blessed to experience.

Along the way to that window, Ruth and I enjoyed some days of great joy and deep fulfillment, but we also endured times when life was dark and difficult. There were detours and disappointments. Through it all, we came to know God's love was real and his grace sufficient for every trial. When I say we came to know God's love was real and his grace sufficient, I'm talking about the kind of knowing that happens when you've walked through life's hard stuff with someone.

Maybe your road hasn't always been an easy one either. You've had good days, but you've also struggled through times of loneliness, depression, or anxiety. Maybe a devastating loss, a heartache, or a disappointment has robbed you of the life you were counting on. Lately, it seems many are on a hard road. Here's something you need to know about painful circumstances: They can talk us into believing something about ourselves or about God that isn't true. In our despair, believing a myth, we find ourselves in darkness, searching for hope. It's a perilous place to be. Without the light of truth, the hope we need to live eludes us.

There was a quote in giant script on the auditorium wall when I went through survival, evasion, resistance, and escape (SERE) training as a young combat flight crew officer near Spokane, Washington. I've not forgotten it. "You can live forty days without food, four days without water, and four minutes without air. But you can't live four seconds without hope." Maybe there's a bit of hyperbole in that, but we know the idea is true. We can't live without hope.

Years ago, when I deployed to Prince Sultan Air Base in the Arabian Desert, our team of chaplains and chaplain assistants had the opportunity to name the chapel that served the five thousand Americans assigned there. We came up with something we thought was perfect and sent a request for the commander's approval to name it Desert Hope Chapel.

The commander didn't care for that name. I'm sure he'd heard it said more than once in his military training that hope is not a plan. When you're briefing the commander on some proposed new course of action, you never start with, "We hope to do this or that . . ." To him, it must have sounded like the Chapel of Uncertainty or the Chapel of We Hope So, but We're Not Sure. I paid a visit to the commander, "hoping" to convince him that the biblical concept of hope was a worthy name for the chapel.

Being the great leader he was, he listened to the dissenting voice. Being the man of faith he was, he understood that the hope God offers us is not wishful thinking dependent on ever-changing and uncertain circumstances. It is a rock-solid confidence built on God's unchanging character. He agreed to the name.

The "dirt boys" in the Civil Engineering Squadron found us the perfect rock to place in front of the chapel. A talented airman fabricated large metal letters and attached them to the flat side of the rock. A front loader delivered the massive stone to the site and set it up for us. We were in business as the Desert Hope Chapel.

Our team of chaplains and chaplain assistants at Prince Sultan Air Base, Saudi Arabia. I'm standing on the far right.

Through the years, thousands of airmen from several nations entered those doors parched, dry, and weary. Inside, they found an oasis in the desert. They were welcomed as family. They were refreshed with grace. They were liberated with truth. They found hope.

Let me tell you my twofold purpose in writing this book. First, wherever you are today, whatever you're going through, my mission is to offer you a taste of hope that will revive you and give you the strength you need to take the next step. Second, my prayer is that, refreshed by hope, you might offer an oasis for someone else on a hard road.

I invite you to read on and drink in the hope that bubbles from the stories I share. As you do, dare to ask God to reveal his truth to you. In the light of that truth, ask God to heal the wounds of your past, give you the strength you need for today, encourage you with the hope of a better day coming, and give you a renewed sense of purpose for living. Would you make that your prayer as you begin this book? Let me suggest you invite a friend or group to read these eleven chapters along with you.

Use them as a springboard to talk about your own story and the story God is writing.

At the end of chapters 1 through 10, I give you a clear reason you can be sure God is for you regardless of the circumstances. There is a prayer you can make your own as you talk to God about what you've just read. Following the prayer, there are a few questions you can use in small group discussion or for processing in your journal. I also share some inspirational songs from my playlist—each one lifts my spirit. As you finish each chapter, take a moment to think about something that spoke to you, and let the music help you meditate on the truth that God is for you.

Chapter 1

THE GOD WHO NEVER SLEEPS

I'm absolutely convinced that nothing—nothing living or dead, angelic or demonic, today or tomorrow, high or low, thinkable or unthinkable—absolutely nothing can get between us and God's love because of the way that Jesus our Master has embraced us.

Romans 8:38–39 MSG

I lay flat on my back in the middle of what's usually a busy two-lane road. The scorching August sun had set more than an hour before, but the asphalt beneath me still radiated heat. Even so, I shivered uncontrollably. I knew I was in shock. The Self-Aid and Buddy Care training every airman receives kicked in and I asked for the blue wool blanket from my Air Force days that I kept in the trunk of my car. An officer standing nearby found the blanket and laid it over me.

Moments before, someone had forced my car door open and eased me out from behind the crushed steering wheel. When I was out of the car and nearly upright, he saw my right foot was pointed in the wrong direction. "Lay him down!" he shouted to his partner.

The blanket lay over me with comforting warmth. My trembling subsided, and the stabbing pain in my leg eased. From my vantage point, the flashing lights reflecting on my car revealed a forest of legs gathering around me. Two EMTs appeared and knelt beside me, immobilizing my right leg with a splint. Soon we'd be on our way to John Peter Smith Hospital in Fort Worth, Texas.

It had happened in the blink of an eye. The only warning was a twitch in the oncoming headlights a split second before the head-on collision. I had no time to brake or to brace myself. The impact left me stunned but still conscious. The moment of collision would replay in my dreams for years.

Our evening had started out as a much-needed getaway from the grind of school and work. Ruth and I had invited another seminary couple to join us and our precocious five-year-old daughter to see an amateur production at one of the large churches in town. After the play and a stop at McDonald's for ice cream, our big night out was done. We headed home to our little fixer-upper just twenty minutes south of the city. Little did I know it would be two months before I'd make it home.

A nurse, also on her way home, arrived at the scene shortly after the crash. Our angel of mercy, whose name I still don't know, left her car and climbed into the ambulance with our daughter Annie. She rode to the emergency room with her, comforting our frightened little girl, who had blood streaming down her face. Annie's mom and I were not able to be with her, but she wasn't alone.

In the ER, my clothes were cut off and I watched as a metal rod was drilled through my leg below the knee. The doctor determined my right femur had snapped in two in a jagged break. So the plan was to put me in traction, hanging a weight at the foot of the bed to pull the ends of the broken femur apart and allow bone material to fill in and mend the break.

Two young men in scrubs wheeled me out of the ER with my leg hoisted in traction. Just before that, I'd heard a report that Ruth and our friends would be okay, and I signed a document approving surgery for our daughter, to repair a cut just below her eye. (She wears a scar there to this day.)

My family arrived from Louisiana the next afternoon. When they spoke to me, my responses didn't make much sense. They called for a nurse. An X-ray revealed that bits of fat had entered my bloodstream from the broken femur and traveled to my lungs. I spent the next fifty hours on a machine that helped me breathe, dead to the world in the intensive care unit. For me, it was one long night. I'm sure I looked pitiable and alone there in my ICU cubicle. Some may have looked at me and wondered whether God had me in time-out. Maybe they were curious what I had done wrong to have God punish me like that. To others, it may have appeared God had simply abandoned me. Nothing could have been further from the truth.

Maybe life has knocked you down. In your pain, you hear a voice telling you that you have no choice but to face this battle alone. Even worse, feelings of guilt and shame or a sense of unworthiness you may have harbored in your heart for years can make you especially vulnerable to believing that God is against you. Don't let your pain and hard circumstances talk you into believing something that isn't true. Anger, especially the kind we turn on ourselves, can isolate us from the help we need from God and others. And then few things can be as deadly as the pride that says, "I don't need God's help or anyone else's."

David was a guy who seemed to process his hard times by songwriting. It was a great way for him to identify the problem, clarify and voice his feelings, and most importantly, to review what he knew to be true. Imagine for a moment what crisis he was in when he wrote the song we know as Psalm 121. We know there were times he was running for his life from treacherous enemies. He struggled with a rebellious son. There were times he descended into deep depression and felt like he had been abandoned. Where was he and what was he facing when he wrote the song with the iconic words "I lift up my eyes to the mountains" (v. 1)? What was the trouble that caused him to scan the distant mountains, searching for an escape? Was he in agony when he cried out, "Where does my help come from?" Can you identify with that?

Maybe you feel so hurt, so afraid, so trapped that you just want to be somewhere else? You want to escape to a safe place, to head for the hills, as David's words suggest. You want to be anywhere other than the place you are now. Maybe you've cried in agony, feeling like no one can truly understand what you're going through. Sometimes, even though others are around you, you feel like you're on your own. May I ask what's got you hunkered down in fear? Or what has caused you to withdraw in anger? Has something traumatic caused you to doubt God's love for you? As you read David's words, drink in this life-changing truth: There is a God who sees you. There is a God who is for you. That just may be the water your battle-weary, bone-dry soul needs right now to live.

> I lift up my eyes to the mountains—
>   where does my help come from?
> My help comes from the LORD,
>   the Maker of heaven and earth.
>
> He will not let your foot slip—
>   he who watches over you will not slumber;
> indeed, he who watches over Israel
>   will neither slumber nor sleep.
>
> The LORD watches over you—
>   The LORD is your shade at your right hand;
> the sun will not harm you by day,
>   nor the moon by night.

> The LORD will keep you from all harm—
> he will watch over your life;
> the LORD will watch over your coming and going
> both now and forevermore.
> (Psalm 121)

David's words are three thousand years old. Yet they're still fresh with hope. On a tough day in my life, they revived me like a bottle of cold, crisp sparkling water on a hot and humid Houston day.

Don't gloss over David's poetic language. What is the essential truth he wanted us to take away? He wanted us to see the priceless benefit of knowing and trusting God in every circumstance—especially the painful, scary ones. David shared the truth he experienced in his own life not just as a statement of fact but as an appeal. When a tsunami of pain or grief hits us and we're in danger of being ripped away from the faith that has been our anchor, his words invite us to take refuge in God's constant care so we can stand our ground and shout the truth to the storm raging around us or the fear lurking within us: "I am not alone!" We can say, "My help comes from the LORD, the Maker of heaven and earth" (v. 2)! Why not post that on your social media or write it on a card and place it somewhere you'll see every day? Make it the home screen on your phone. Or best of all, do what David did when God shared a truth with him: Memorize it. "I have hidden your word in my heart that I might not sin against you" (119:11).

Switching from his story to ours, David added, "The sun will not harm you by day, nor the moon by night" (121:6). The poet was saying that 24/7, God is with you. Through the heat of the day, God is with you. And all through the lonely night hours when we feel most vulnerable, God is still there. But there's more. David wasn't just saying God watches over us every hour. He was also telling us God cares about every good, bad, and ugly detail of our lives. He is always there with the help only he can give.

As young parents, we always did our best to keep an eye on

our kids, but there were times they wore us out. I'm enjoying watching some young friends experience the joys of adjusting to life with their first child. They welcomed a beautiful little girl into their lives several months ago. Immediately, baby Sawyer took charge of their schedules. To their dismay, this sweet child with an angelic face loves the nightlife. Mom and Dad are probably not safe to operate machinery right now. If you've been there, you understand.

> **God cares about every good, bad, and ugly detail of our lives. He is always there with the help only he can give.**

There are pictures of me meeting our firstborn. I laugh when I see them. Our daughter, Anne, was seven days old when I made it home from the Air Force SERE school in Washington state, which included prisoner of war (POW) camp training (yes, there's a school for that). I had left immediately after my experience as a prisoner in the POW camp, running a serious sleep deficit. In the pictures of our first day together, I'm holding our new baby girl with my chin on my chest. As excited as I was to be a new dad, I could not keep my eyes open. Annie and I were both sleeping peacefully.

Not so with God. "He . . . will neither slumber nor sleep," the poet assured us (Psalm 121:4). There's never a moment when you're out of his sight. There's never a moment when God does not care. No cloud can hide you and no distraction can keep you from his watchful care. In fact, nothing can separate you from God's love and care. Try speaking these words out loud right now: Nothing can separate me from God's love! Not this disease. Not this divorce. Not this darkness. Not even this doubt. Absolutely nothing.

How did David know that? He knew because he had lived that truth. When he was a shepherd boy guarding his father's sheep, he learned God was with him day and night. He remembered how he had rescued a sheep from the jaws of a lion with God's help. He could never forget how he defeated a giant with God's help, using a slingshot and a precision-guided rock. Through the ups and downs in his life, David had come to know that God was watching over him with continuous, unblinking care, even when his painful circumstances might have tempted him to believe that God was against him. The death of a child and the rebellion of a son could not pull him from the truth that anchored his soul. In this pain and in this loss, he could still say, "My help comes from the LORD, the Maker of heaven and earth" (v. 2).

THE ORDEAL

When I read David's words, "He who watches over you will not slumber" (v. 3), I'm reminded of an unforgettable experience I had as a Boy Scout. As a Scout progresses through the ranks from Tenderfoot toward Eagle, he may be invited to join the Order of the Arrow. I accepted such an invitation and showed up at the camp with my gear ready for the induction weekend, aptly named the "Ordeal."

The Ordeal began that night with a group of us boys sitting wide-eyed around a blazing bonfire. A leader stood and spoke firmly to us. "Beginning now, you may not speak until the Ordeal is complete. Line up!"

There was a long rope to define the line. Each boy grabbed the rope with his left hand. I took my place in the middle. Without a word, the rope started pulling us forward. Step by step, we moved farther away from the circle of light. Entering the dark woods, we followed a narrow, winding trail until it disappeared. Still, the rope pulled us on. Now there were only the night sounds of the woods and our feet shuffling in the rustling leaves, which I noticed were becoming fainter behind me. As we walked on in silence, I realized I was now the tail end of the line.

That was when a hand gripped my shoulder, pulling me from the line, which soon disappeared into the woods without me. A dark silhouette pointed to a spot on the ground. I decided that was where I was supposed to stay.

The silhouette turned to walk away. "Good night," I heard myself blurt out. It seemed the right thing to say at the time.

The silhouette stopped. He turned toward me and took something from his pocket. I stood rooted to the ground. He reached toward me and took hold of the bamboo with the cotton cord threaded through it, which he had hung around my neck when we sat by the fire. A knife blade flashed open. He cut a notch in the bamboo and spoke in a stern voice. "Do. Not. Speak."

Years later, I met a member of the Cherokee tribe who spoke with pride about the culture of his people. He shared the story of an early tribal rite of passage for boys on their way to becoming men. He told us how the men of the village would lead the boys into the woods and leave them alone in the darkness to wait for morning, their ears alert to every movement in the leaves and every wild creature's call.

My face lit up. "I know this story!"

Then my friend came to the best part of his story. After the long, frightful night in the dark woods, the first light of day revealed something wonderful the boy would never forget. All through the night his father had been there standing guard, watching over him. He hadn't been alone at all.

With the ordeal our family went through when a head-on collision nearly ended my life, it would have been easy to look at our circumstances and think we were alone in a dark place. When you find yourself in an ICU room with a poor prognosis, you may come to a false conclusion. During eight weeks in traction, unable to care for your family, you might be tempted to tell yourself something that's not true. Wherever your dark night happens to be—a hospital room, a prison cell, or a dinner table with an empty chair—you may be tempted to despair and cry out, "God, have you abandoned me?"

Regardless of what your circumstances may lead you to believe, you're not alone. Your heavenly Father is watching over you, just as he was watching over David. Even in your suffering, you can be sure he is still for you.

Ruth and I knew a former Air Force doctor who was serving at the hospital where I was in the ICU. While stationed in the San Francisco Bay Area several years before, we had attended the same church and become friends with the good doctor and his wife, Rosemary. After I was moved to the ICU, Dr. Bill Singleton somehow found the time to drive out to Crowley to visit with Ruth. He and our pastor sat next to each other by Ruth's bed, where she was propped up with several pillows.

You're not alone. Your heavenly Father is watching over you.

"It doesn't look good for Bob," Dr. Singleton said to her. "But youth is on his side."

He added this bit of encouragement to an otherwise bleak situation. Then he asked her whether I had life insurance and if she knew where that paperwork was.

Several friends heard what had happened to us. When the word reached them that I was in critical condition, they gathered at our church on a Sunday night to pray for me. I'll tell it to you exactly as it happened. The next morning, there was no evidence of the life-threatening emboli that had sent me to the ICU.

Later, I heard of someone who died of a pulmonary embolism on the very same day I recovered. That brings us to a difficult question, doesn't it? I wish I could tell you why God says yes to some prayers and not others. What I can tell you is that God loved the one who lived and the one who died. You may also be thinking, *If God is for us and watching over us, why does he allow bad things to happen to us?* I agree that's an obvious question—and I've saved that discussion for chapter 8.

LIKE MANNA FROM HEAVEN

Returning to my room, I lay on my back with my right leg hanging from the frame over the bed. I had a family depending on me. For the first time in my adult life, I had no income, and I could do nothing about that. I had just registered for my first fall term at seminary and had to drop out before I ever attended the first class. I had paid the tuition using the GI Bill benefits I'd earned during the six years I served in the Air Force.[1] Now, because I wasn't a student, the VA sent a notice for me to return the money.

When I left the security of the Air Force, I had come up with a plan on how to support our family through three years of seminary. I'd taken night classes after we arrived in Fort Worth to prepare for a Texas real estate license. Once I had my license in hand, Martin Hedrick had taken me on as one of the agents in his realty office. While that was incredibly gracious, it was a terrible time for someone to get started in real estate. Mortgage interest rates had been climbing for the past year and hit 16 percent about the time I showed up at the office.

Despite the sky-high interest rates and my lack of experience in real estate, somehow I listed two houses for sale that summer. Then the accident happened. Back in the office, seasoned agents were hustling and drinking antacid straight from the bottle, trying to move houses. Despite their best efforts, beautiful homes in desirable locations sat on the market month after month. Now, I couldn't even show the two houses I had listed. Amazingly, against all odds, one of the houses I'd listed sold the first month I was in the hospital. Mr. Hedrick brought my wife a check for my share of the commission. The next month, the second house sold. Mr. Hedrick delivered a second check. It was like manna from heaven!

Pain was my most frequent visitor, especially during my first month in traction. The worst was when the muscles around the broken femur would spasm, causing excruciating pain. Thankfully, this didn't happen every day, and it became less frequent as the weeks dragged by.

I only share that to caution you not to misinterpret Psalm 121. God doesn't promise you'll never suffer pain, struggle through hard times, or experience loss. David, the songwriter who wrote the words to Psalm 121, experienced all those things in his life. Consider that Jesus himself suffered the agony and indignity of a criminal's death on a cross. Not only that, but through the centuries, many of the men and women who followed Jesus suffered greatly. In fact, early evidence indicates ten of Jesus's disciples, who were witnesses to his resurrection, chose to die as martyrs rather than deny what they knew to be true.[2] Before the trauma of the cross, Jesus prepared his friends for the hard times he knew were coming for them by saying, "Blessed are you when people insult you, persecute you and falsely say all kinds of evil against you because of me. Rejoice and be glad, because great is your reward in heaven" (Matthew 5:11–12).

Whatever Psalm 121 means, it doesn't mean a young man driving drunk won't hit us head-on one night on a two-lane road.

So what *does* it mean? It means whatever you're going through, you don't have to go through it alone. God is there with you in your pain, your sorrow, and your struggle. It means there's nothing this world can throw at you that the Maker of heaven and earth can't rescue you from, help you with, heal you of, and bring you through victorious. With God, hope is always a reasonable response to what we're going through. Even our old enemy death doesn't have the last word when God is with you. Irish poet and hymn writer Thomas Moore put it like this, "Earth has no sorrow that heaven cannot heal."[3] David Crowder borrowed those hope-filled words for his song "Come as You Are."[4]

I don't know what you think about God or whether you even believe in God, but here's what the eyewitnesses to Jesus's resurrection believed: If you want to see what God is really like, look at Jesus. When we look at him, we see things about God that can change everything for us if we'll receive them.

"Show us the Father and that will be enough for us," one of Jesus's followers requested (John 14:8).

Jesus told him, "Anyone who has seen me has seen the Father"

(v. 9). So here's the truth: Jesus helps us see that God is not only the almighty Maker of heaven and earth, far above us. He's also One who is *with* us, a loving Father who cares for us. That's the God who is watching over you.

DOWN ON THE TRACK

Derek Redmond was favored to win the men's four-hundred-meter race in the 1992 Olympics in Barcelona, Spain. When the gun sounded, he launched well. He was running smoothly when he heard a snap and felt a sharp pain in his leg about fifteen seconds into the race. He went down hard on the track with a hamstring injury.

What happened next is my favorite Olympic moment of all time. There was no way now that Derek would finish this race with a gold, silver, or even a bronze medal, but he was determined that he would finish. He rose from the track and hobbled and hopped toward the finish line in a magnificent demonstration of perseverance. With the world watching through misty eyes, he struggled to keep going. The camera was not focused on the winner now but on Derek Redmond. Even though he was in pain, he simply would not quit.

A commotion started on the sideline. Someone was pushing his way onto the track—Derek's father. He was present at the race, watching his son with the pride and love only a parent knows. Jim Redmond reached his son and put his arm around him. He walked with him, and together they crossed the finish line.[5]

I don't know what you're struggling through. Maybe in your disappointment or pain, you feel like God has abandoned you or that he's against you. If that's where you are, my heart goes out to you. That's a hard place to be. But I want you to know there is a God who loves you, a heavenly Father who is still for you. You don't have to suffer or grieve alone. He wants to come alongside you and be the help you need right now.

When I was my most helpless, the Lord helped me. When I had no way to care for myself or my family, he cared for us and supplied our need. When I was knocked down, in my weakness I trusted him and found strength beyond my own. Whatever you're going through, lean into him. Trust him to walk with you and give you what you need to make it through this day.

Here's what I know is true: Your heavenly Father is watching over you. He sees you down on the track. He's there to help you. He'll be the strength you need. Reach up for help. Leaning on him, you can go on and finish this race. Trust him. He is still for you.

You can be sure God is for you because . . .

God is always watching over you.

PRAYER

Lord, despite what my circumstances may lead me to believe, despite the pain I feel right now, the truth is, you are for me. I know you see what I'm going through, and you care about me. Right now I choose to trust you. Thank you that nothing in my past, present, or future can ever separate me from your love. I pray this in Jesus's name. Amen.

TALK IT OVER

1. Describe a time you questioned your faith because of something that happened (or is happening) to you or someone you love.

2. David wrote, "My help comes from the LORD, the Maker of heaven and earth" (Psalm 121:2). Where do you need God's help now?

3. What would you say to encourage someone who feels they are alone going through a difficult situation?

A SONG TO LIFT YOUR SPIRIT

"Hold on to Me" by Lauren Daigle

Chapter 2

ROADBLOCKS AND DETOURS

In all things God works for the good of those who love him, who have been called according to his purpose.

Romans 8:28

These days, we live on the southwest side of Houston and make regular trips to Louisiana to visit my family. On one such trip, we sailed through Houston, and the eastbound traffic on I-10 flowed along smoothly. I thought, *We'll make it to Baton Rouge by midafternoon.* Everything was going exactly as we had planned. Perfect!

But in my experience, you never travel eastbound on I-10 from Houston to Baton Rouge exactly as planned. There's always road construction, a delay, or a detour. The fifty-seven-year-old bottleneck—still known as "the new bridge"—spanning the

Mississippi River with only one eastbound lane can be an adventure by itself. If that's not your experience, I want to ride with you next time you're headed that way.

I guess at times we've all bought into the false notion that if we've got some beautiful, worthy destination in life's GPS, God is supposed to clear all the roadblocks and there won't be a need to recalculate along the way. The trouble with that idea is that when the inevitable roadblocks and detours do happen—especially with some cherished dream we thought was from God—we find ourselves confused, discouraged, and questioning what we believed about God. When we find ourselves stalled in a long, narrow parking lot we thought was a high-speed highway to our dream, we ask, "God, where are you now? I thought you were for me!"

I WON THE LOTTERY!

I served as a chaplain in the United States Air Force for more than twenty-five years. But long before I was a chaplain, I went through a year of Undergraduate Navigator Training after college, then served five years as an Air Force navigator on a KC-135A—a big four-engine aircraft built to carry cargo and troops and do one other job essential to national security. The KC-135's primary mission was refueling fighters, bombers, and reconnaissance aircraft in-flight. Think of it as a flying gas station.

I never planned to be a navigator or a chaplain. In fact, I never planned to be in the military at all. One day toward the end of my first year at Louisiana State University, I realized God had a special purpose for my life. I was pretty sure he wanted me to be a missionary. It was a beautiful thing that brought such clarity to my life. I had a plan. I knew where I was headed. I was on my way! I'll never forget that day.

I was a music education major my first year at LSU. One morning I was sequestered in a small practice room on the second floor of the music building. There was enough space for a piano, a piano bench, and me. I'm sure I was supposed to be sawing away at scales or arpeggios, torturing some poor violin that morning. Instead, the violin case sat unopened at my feet. I had something I wanted to do first. My Bible was open to a passage in the New Testament book of Acts.

Thanks to my pastor, daily Bible reading was a good habit I picked up in a small group that had been meeting weekly for several years. My pastor during my teen years was affectionately known to his flock as Brother Wilkinson. He was a short, energetic man with a round face that was home to a perpetual smile. During a meeting in his study one afternoon, he suggested that several of us form a small group and call it "Spiritual Interchange." Let me help you see the beauty of his idea. When spoken with a fully developed, well-formed Southern accent, "interchange" sounds like "inner change," creating a marvelous and meaningful word play. I'm smiling now. I hope you are too.

His idea was that each of us would read our Bibles and pray daily. Then we'd come together on Friday evenings to share what we had learned. Through our interchange there would be the opportunity for *inner* change. I think it was my first encounter with the idea that a thriving spiritual life is more than a "me and Jesus" deal. It's a team sport. Truth is, we all need a team. It doesn't matter where or what the challenge is—we need others. When life is hard and you're looking for hope, find your team.

The change we're desperate to see in our lives can happen when we build enough trust to be transparent with another person, when we allow someone to know us and love us as we are. Here's another thing that fuels life change: being willing to move our focus beyond ourselves to the needs and interests of others. It just so happens those are two of the very things that can happen in a small group.

As I read from Acts that day in the music room, I was gripped with a sudden and powerful impression. That's the only way I can describe what happened. The words I read were simply Luke (the writer of Luke and Acts) telling the story of how, at the Spirit's direction, the church sent out two characters named

Barnabas and Saul on a mission. They were to go out from Antioch and bear witness to the good news of Jesus (Acts 13:1–3).

> **A thriving spiritual life is more than a "me and Jesus" deal. It's a team sport.**

Somehow I realized I also had a mission. I would leave home to bear witness to the good news. I had no idea where or when or how, but there was no doubt in my mind that God was calling me to a special purpose, not in an audible voice but with an undeniable impression I've never doubted for more than fifty years.

I met with Brother Wilkinson and told him what I had experienced in the practice room. Of course, I also told our Friday night Spiritual Interchange group what had happened. My busy pastor did a truly generous thing. I don't know that I fully appreciated the extraordinary gift he gave me at the time, but I certainly do now. He took a full day out of his schedule and invited me and the pastor of the church I'd attended as a child to ride with him to the seminary in New Orleans, where he'd arranged for me to talk with Dr. Herndon, the dean of students. Not only that, but he also encouraged me and gave me opportunities to serve and lead in various ministries that let me test the call I had experienced in the music practice room. As I served and encountered challenges, he offered wise counsel and gentle correction. He connected me with the people who could help me with the next steps in my journey. Those are the things effective mentors do. Who I am today is a direct result of the timely and priceless investment of this selfless, humble pastor in my life.

With each person I spoke to, my next step became clearer. With each bit of encouragement and affirmation, I became even more confident I was on the right track. Perfect!

What I know now that I didn't then is you never travel through life exactly as planned. The next year, a major recalculation happened. I won the lottery! The draft lottery, that is. Along with all the other young men born on December 12, 1951, I was entitled to a free, highly invasive medical exam and an all-expenses-paid trip to exotic locations.

How could this be happening? I had been so confident. I had God and life all figured out, as only an eighteen-year-old can. Didn't everyone I spoke to give me a glowing, positive response? Didn't they all tell me they'd expected this for some time? Then this huge roadblock. It was confusing, to say the least. I checked, and there were no deferments for college students with a plan to graduate, go to seminary, and launch a mission to save the world. (I'm smiling again.) What was I to do?

Someone suggested a detour. I found my way to a nondescript brick building near Tiger Stadium and had my first encounter with military acronyms. Military folks have never met an acronym they didn't love. I walked to the AFROTC building, where I took the AFOQT. For those who don't speak military, that's the Air Force Reserve Officer Training Corps and the Air Force Officer Qualification Test.

The results of the test showed I was qualified to serve as an officer and that I had an aptitude for navigation. Who knew? At this same time, the number of US forces in Vietnam was approaching nearly a half million troops, and the war was demanding an ever-increasing level of air support. The Air Force was in need of navigators. You do the math.

The officer across the desk explained, "We'll let you in our two-year Air Force ROTC program if you agree to be a navigator candidate."

I could finish the degree I would need to attend seminary someday and graduate on time. That was important. I would be commissioned the day after graduation as a lieutenant in the Air Force. Bonus. But there was a hitch.

Instead of being drafted into the Army for four years (as was typical back then), I'd have to commit to a year of navigator training plus five years of active-duty service in the Air Force. Six years! At the tender age of eighteen, that seemed like a lifetime away.

So these were my options: I could be drafted and serve four

years. Or I could finish college and incur a six-year commitment to the Air Force. Shouldn't I get through this detour and get back on my planned route as quickly as possible? I went home to think about it and pray. I have to admit I was confused. I thought about the promise I had learned as a child.

> Trust in the LORD with all your heart
> and lean not on your own understanding;
> in all your ways submit to him,
> and he will make your paths straight.
> (Proverbs 3:5–6)

I had memorized these verses as a kid. I wanted to believe them, but this sure seemed like a great big, crooked detour. "God, wasn't I trusting you and submitting to you? Where's that straight path you promised?"

That night at home, I read from Matthew. I paused when I came to Matthew 5:41. I had recently learned the background on this verse from Jesus's Sermon on the Mount and realized it was apropos to my situation.

In Jesus's day, Rome maintained an occupying military force in Israel. Then and now, when a military unit moves, a ton of stuff must move with the troops. In my days on a combat flight crew, we called it a *bag drag*. Rome allowed its soldiers to force the local men to help with their bag drag. But their law limited how far a soldier could require a civilian to carry his stuff. They could legally make you carry their burden one mile.[1] Even with this limitation, I'm sure those young men resented being treated like foreign soldiers' pack animals. Well, think of it: Besides the Romans being a foreign occupying army, when is it ever convenient for someone to disrupt your plans and impose their need on you, even if it is just for a mile?

Jesus had some radical instructions for these men who hated carrying the Roman soldiers' stuff. He said, "If a soldier demands that you carry his gear for a mile, carry it two miles" (Matthew 5:41 NLT).

Well, the principle certainly fit my situation. So I set out to go the second mile on what I thought would be a long six-year detour. You may question my application of the verse, but I have to say that decision has made all the difference in my life. Today, I'm grateful to God for that timely verse and the way he led me to go the second mile.

By the way, I've discovered going the extra mile is also a formula for success in life. Try going the second mile for your spouse, friend, customer, or boss. It's just a good principle in life to give more than is expected. Start at home and give it a try.

Going the extra mile is also a formula for success in life. Try going the second mile for your spouse, friend, customer, or boss.

You know, if Jesus had been offering this advice to my Cajun friends and family, it might have sounded like this: "*Cher*, I guarantee, *lagniappe c'est si bon*!"

My folks in southern Louisiana know *lagniappe* is getting a little something extra you didn't expect, like a golden-brown hush puppy with your fried catfish or a sweet pecan praline for dessert. And you know, that's a good thing!

Don't think for a minute I could see what God was doing. I was just holding on to his promise. According to Proverbs 3:5–6, if I would trust him and follow his leading even when I didn't understand, he would make a straight path of my life. I was learning a valuable lesson. When you can't comprehend God's ways, choose to trust God's character.

That's precisely the message of Psalm 9:10: "*Those who know your name* trust in you, for you, Lord, have never forsaken those who seek you." In Scripture, a person's name is not just something you call them by. To know their name is to know their character. When you've experienced the grace and the goodness of God, you begin to know something about his character.

DON'T FORGET THE *CHESED*!

There's a beautiful Hebrew word that's almost untranslatable, certainly not in a single English word. It's the word *chesed* (rhymes with *bless-ed*). When it's used for God's love for us, it's sometimes rendered "unfailing love," "mercy," or "loving-kindness." For example, the New International Version (NIV) uses "unfailing love" to translate *chesed* in Psalm 13:5. David poured out his heart with extraordinary transparency in Psalm 13. In his deep sorrow and struggle, what is it that inspired his trust through difficult circumstances? *Chesed*! God's unfailing love.

> How long, LORD? Will you forget me forever?
> How long will you hide your face from me?
> How long must I wrestle with my thoughts
> and day after day have sorrow in my heart?
> How long will my enemy triumph over me?
>
> Look on me and answer, LORD my God.
> Give light to my eyes, or I will sleep in death,
> and my enemy will say, "I have overcome him,"
> and my foes will rejoice when I fall.
>
> But I trust in your *unfailing love* [*chesed*];
> my heart rejoices in your salvation.
> I will sing the LORD's praise,
> for he has been good to me."
>
> (Psalm 13)

In Psalm 36:7 the New King James Version translates *chesed* as "lovingkindness": "How precious is Your *lovingkindness*, O God! Therefore the children of men put their trust under the shadow of Your wings." I love that image. People who have experienced the extravagance of God's loving-kindness trust him. They take refuge and rest safe and secure, like chicks sheltered underneath the wings of their mother.

In both Psalm 13:5 and Psalm 36:7, it was God's unfailing love that made the difference. In his trouble in Psalm 13, David felt abandoned and depressed. He felt that without God's intervention, he was headed for defeat and death. Yet despite all that, David chose to trust God. Why should he trust God at a time when it sounds like his life was so miserable?

Here's why: In days past, he had experienced God's goodness. He had tasted the *chesed* of God, and he would never forget how God had been good to him, far beyond what he should expect. He remembered how God had forgiven him and not treated him as his sins deserved. Instead, God had shown him mercy and grace. He remembered how God had protected him. He called to mind how God had provided for him. What he knew of the character of God made it possible for him to trust God even when life was hard.

Chesed is God's faithful love, grace, and mercy lavished on us, not because of anything we've done to deserve it but because God has chosen to do so in Christ.[2] Here's the amazing part—he has done this with full knowledge of who we are and all we've done.

We have to think beyond our ideas of romantic love or human affection. *Chesed* isn't about my being so doggone lovable God just can't help himself. God's love for each of us originates entirely in himself. It is the strong will of God that takes the initiative and sacrifices to rescue the objects of his love—you and me. Paul said it like this, "God demonstrates his own love for us in this: While we were still sinners, Christ died for us" (Romans 5:8). I want you to hear that verse written for you. Read it again out loud, and this time make it personal. "God demonstrates his own love for *me* in this: While *I* was still a sinner, Christ died for *me*."

Here's the point. When you have experienced a love like *chesed*, you know you can trust God even when circumstances are confusing. So try this: When you don't understand God's ways, trust his heart. If unexpected, unwanted things have happened or discouraging delays have made your life a spiritual desert, I guarantee trusting God through the disappointment and uncertainty will lead you to an oasis.

GOT PATIENCE?

When our six-year detour was over, Ruth and I packed up and left California for Fort Worth, Texas, where I enrolled in seminary. When the day came for us to give up our military ID cards, I have to admit it was scary. Those ID cards had been the ticket to all our military benefits, including a salary and health care. After six years it was easy to think they were the source of our security. At the same time, it felt good to get back on track.

After three years of full-time school and working a job (including the semester I spent in the hospital and at home recovering from the accident), I graduated from seminary and was called to pastor a church in Arkansas. From the day I first felt God call me to ministry in a music practice room at LSU to the day I stood before a congregation as their pastor was thirteen years.

The message here is this: Don't give up and drop out when life doesn't load as fast as you want it to. Sometimes we expect life to run on high-speed internet. In my experience, it seldom works like that. Be patient when that education, job, dream, marriage, or healing doesn't happen as quickly as you think it should. In case you haven't noticed, God's perspective on time is different from ours. This is one of life's most valuable lessons. Wouldn't you love to know how the apostle Peter was introduced to this truth? He said, "Do not forget this one thing, dear friends: With the Lord a day is like a thousand years, and a thousand years are like a day" (2 Peter 3:8).

A PATH MADE STRAIGHT

After three years serving a church in northwest Arkansas, I was called to lead a growing congregation in the beautiful hills of western North Carolina. I had been there three years when, early one morning, my phone rang. A man identified himself and moved to the reason for his call. "Bob, we can put one chaplain on active duty in the Air Force this year. We'd like to include your name in our selection process. Would you be interested?"

It was Lew Burnett calling from his office in Atlanta at the North American Mission Board (formerly known as the Home Mission Board). Their organization was responsible for endorsing chaplains from our denomination to serve each military branch. My name was on their current roster of endorsees because I was serving as a chaplain in the Air Force Reserve. While I was a full-time pastor in North Carolina, I would put the uniform back on and serve two weeks each summer and two days a month alongside active-duty chaplains at Shaw Air Force Base in South Carolina.

Lew explained the process in his soft Texas drawl, and I respectfully declined. I was totally invested where I was, and my heart was in the work I was doing. A week later Lew called again, and once again I turned him down. Even though I thought I had given him my final answer, this persistent man called back a third time. He encouraged me to reconsider. "Bob, why don't you and Ruth come to Atlanta to talk with us about this?"

Lew and I were on familiar terms by this time, so I spoke frankly. "Lew, before I waste your time and mine, let me talk with Ruth again and pray together about this tonight. I'll call you back in the morning."

After the children were in bed, Ruth and I talked for some time. My sweet wife told me she loved where we were, but she was willing to go if that's what God wanted us to do. Here's what's so amazing about that: Ruth had grown up in an Air Force family. She knew what it was like to move every three years and say goodbye to friends and try to fit into a new place. There were several times when that had been really hard for her. She told me she had always longed for a hometown, and our current ministry in Franklin, North Carolina, about two hours north of Atlanta, felt like home to her. We prayed together for God's guidance, and she went on to bed. Later I sat with my Bible open in my lap, trying to think through this big decision that would have a huge impact on the church, my wife, our children, and me. A verse came to mind. Who wants to guess what that verse was? If you guessed Matthew 5:41, you'd be right. "If a soldier demands that you carry his gear for a mile, carry it two miles" (NLT).

When I finally opened my mind to the idea, I was able to see the obvious. God had given me a strong and capable wife, an Air Force chaplain's daughter, whose superpower was her ability to adapt to new situations. That's just the superpower a military spouse needs. Not only that, but she also grew up with a front-row seat to her wonderful mother serving as an able partner in ministry to airmen. It just seemed like her mother was made for that role. Plus, God had given me six years as an Air Force navigator, during which I had learned the language and culture. Ruth and I discovered we loved Air Force people. (Still do.) We had come to know firsthand the challenges they face daily.

Suddenly I saw the truth. The idea that I had spent six years on a detour was a big myth. It wasn't a detour at all. God had been preparing me to serve a group of people he loves, to put on their uniform just as Jesus had put on our flesh, to become one of them and fully experience the life they live with its joys and sorrows, and through it all to bear witness to the good news of God's great love for military men and women and their families. It was the perfect preparation. Checking the rearview mirror, the winding road behind us with the unexpected roadblock and detour started to look a lot like a straight path. When faith checks the rearview mirror, it can always see how the Lord has provided and protected and led. That's exactly what I saw that night.

There was something else I discovered: My second mile wasn't six years instead of four. Those six years serving as a navigator were just the first mile. My second mile began in 1989, when we left North Carolina for my assignment to serve as a chaplain at Yokota Air Base, Japan, with an American population of over ten thousand people. Yokota sits just outside Tokyo, and when the conditions are right, it offers a beautiful view of the famed Mount Fuji.

Little did I know that second mile would take me to the Pentagon to serve as the twenty-fourth Air Force deputy chief of chaplains and would end on January 1, 2016, with my retirement from the Air Force. Those three decades serving as a chaplain didn't look anything like what I imagined my life and ministry would be. But those years were more fulfilling and more fruitful than anything I could have planned on my own.

WORKING TOGETHER WITH GOD

Many turn to the words of Romans 8:28 when they're suffering or going through something hard or confusing, and with good reason. In just eighteen Greek words, the promise of something good coming out of our difficulty shines like a beacon of hope through the fog of our circumstances. In some translations the promise is written like this: "In everything *God works* for the good of those who love him" (ERV). In other translations it reads, "*All things work* together for good" (ESV). I think the best understanding of this verse is found in the footnote of the NIV: "Or that *in all things God works together with those who love him* to bring about what is good."[3] Yes, it is God who is working out things for our good, but we are not passive spectators. We are co-laborers with God (1 Corinthians 3:9).

And what is the work God is doing together with us? Oh, it's a wonderful work! It's the work God has had in his heart from the beginning. It is that you and I would experience the life-changing love he demonstrated for us in his son, Jesus. Day by day, going through all the things in our lives—the wonderful things, the terrible things, the things beyond our control, even the messes of our own making—as we cooperate with God and open our hearts to his grace, he transforms us to become more like Jesus. And there's more. Not only does he work with us to clean up the exteriors, getting rid of hurtful, self-destructive behaviors, but he also goes to work on our interiors, renewing our hearts until we love and care for others—and ourselves—more and more like Jesus does. And there's even more. Not only does God enter into a major renovation project with us, but he invites us to work with him in sharing his love with others. He has so many good things he has prepared for us to do (Ephesians 2:10). And there's still more! Through it all, God receives the glory and honor he deserves. That's a whole lot of good that can be accomplished if we will trust God and work together with him in all things.

CHECKING THE REARVIEW MIRROR

Let me speak to the one who's discouraged, confused, or bitter because a big roadblock has appeared between you and the future you envisioned. Maybe you're tempted to give up because life isn't turning out anything like you planned. You had such great intentions and high hopes for your marriage or your career or your cherished dream. Now it seems that dream has been crushed. Maybe something beyond your control has dropped a roadblock in front of you. How could this have happened? It's so unfair. Perhaps you're wondering, *Hey, wasn't God supposed to watch over me and clear the roadblocks out of my way? How can I trust a God who calls me and gives me a work to do, then allows something to block the path?*

I want to encourage you to take a moment and look back. But here's a word of caution as you do. If shame, fear, or anger are riding with you, don't ask any of them to check the rearview mirror. You already know what they'll see. Instead, when you look back, make sure faith is riding with you that day.

Ask faith to check your rearview mirror with you. When faith looks back on the road you've traveled, even with its unexpected stops and turns, you will see how God has helped you and protected you, sometimes in spite of yourself. You'll see God's kindness and mercy. I hope you'll see the priceless gift of forgiveness in Christ that's available to every person for the asking. If you look back and see any of that, no doubt you'll also see that God is for you. During some dry seasons, I've camped in the oasis of remembering what God has done for me in times past, and knowing God is for me.

If somewhere in your life you've had a taste of that loving-kindness of God the ancients called *chesed,* I want you to remember that time and place. Call that moment to mind and decide that going forward you will trust God's heart even if you don't understand his ways. Then take the next step without having to see the whole route. You need to know that God is not going to reveal the whole plan from the beginning. He may choose to show you only the next step. Will you choose to trust God to work through your broken way with all its stops and starts and detours, for your good and for the blessing of others?

> **God is not going to reveal the whole plan from the beginning. He may choose to show you only the next step.**

You probably won't see your life as a straight path from where you stand right now. I understand that. I've been there. But even as painful or confusing as life may seem now, I encourage you to trust the Lord with your whole heart. Don't listen to the voices of doom and gloom. Trust him for all you need. Thank him for all you've been given. Make pleasing him your goal in all you do. And he will lead you to a place where someday you'll look back and see how he has blessed the broken road. When that day comes—and perhaps even now—you'll be able to look up and give thanks to the God of unfailing love.

We believe the prophet Jeremiah wrote the book of Lamentations in the Hebrew Scriptures after he experienced the trauma of the invasion and destruction of Jerusalem. We call him the weeping prophet. As he walked the streets of a once proud city, he lamented the suffering and devastation. Yet in the midst of it all, he looked back and remembered something that gave him hope. What did he see in his rearview mirror?

I will never forget this awful time,
    as I grieve over my loss.
Yet I still dare to hope
    when I remember this:

The faithful love of the LORD never ends!
    His mercies never cease.
Great is His faithfulness;
    his mercies begin afresh each morning.
        (Lamentations 3:20–23 NLT)

You can be sure God is for you when you remember . . .

God has been good to you in the past.

PRAYER

Lord, even though my circumstances right now may be painful and confusing, I remember how you've been good to me. I remember how you've helped me. I remember how you've treated me with grace and kindness at times when I least deserved it. Today I choose to trust you and follow your leading. I believe if I trust and obey, you will help me work together with you through these hard times to accomplish something good in my life and in the lives of others. Through all these circumstances, my heart's desire is that you will receive glory and honor. I pray this in Jesus's name. Amen.

TALK IT OVER

1. Describe a roadblock that stands between you and something dear to you. What can you do to actively trust God in this situation?

2. How has a detour in your life affected your relationship with God?

3. David described a time when he felt like God had abandoned him (Psalm 13). Yet he remembered how God had shown him great kindness in times past and chose to continue trusting in God's unfailing love. Share a time or times in your past when God helped you, blessed you, forgave you, provided for you, or protected you. How was that like the unfailing love (*chesed*) of God that David remembered in his past?

4. How would you encourage someone who is discouraged or confused by an unexpected delay or detour in their life?

SONGS TO LIFT YOUR SPIRIT

"Trust in You" by Lauren Daigle

"Goodness of God" by CeCe Winans

"My Redeemer Is Faithful and True" by Steven Curtis Chapman

Chapter 3

A BRASS COIN AND SOLID-GOLD TRUTH

When I am afraid, I put my trust in you. . . .
What can mere mortals do to me?

David, after he was captured by his enemy (Psalm 56:3–4)

I was traveling in comfortable jeans, slip-off-slip-on TSA-ready shoes, and a shirt with a pocket. I always wear a shirt with a pocket when flying as it's the perfect spot to keep my glasses. The appropriate military uniform for this trip was packed in my checked bag. A young man put what looked to be a new backpack in the bin over my head and took the aisle seat next to me. We chatted a bit before I asked, "Where ya headed?"

When I discovered he was an airman on his way to Afghanistan, I introduced myself. He was amazed, struck by the coincidence that he was headed out on his first deployment and was assigned the seat next to an Air Force chaplain. He let the conversation fly at that point, and I listened from the middle seat. He shared pictures and stories of his entire family, including a mutt who had obviously won the lottery when he was adopted by this young airman and his bride.

After a while, the conversation shifted. I could tell he was anxious about his first deployment. Perhaps the thought crossed his mind that he might not make it home again. But he revealed his greatest concern was not the danger that lay ahead of him in Afghanistan. He was worried about his young wife half a world away at his home base on the island of Okinawa, Japan.

Several months before his departure, they'd found out his wife was pregnant with their first child. They were ecstatic. The problem was that the baby was due to arrive before he would return from his deployment. I could tell this young man loved his wife, and I knew he would be with her if he could, but that wasn't possible. That's why they call those papers that send you to war "orders" and not "invitations." I thought of how my wife had given birth to our first daughter while I was away on orders. So I understood.

I should tell you, I was fulfilling a calling that day as I talked with the airman in the seat next to me. You might say it was a calling within a calling. First, there was that day in the practice room at LSU when I'd discovered God had a special purpose for my life. I didn't know where that calling would take me, but I took a step of faith, and the adventure began. Years later there was a day when I realized that purpose was to care for airmen and their families. I never would have imagined that on my own.

I should also tell you, the military doesn't recruit chaplains so the chaplain can fulfill his or her calling. Chaplains wear the uniform not for themselves but to guarantee the First Amendment rights for every American who serves in the armed forces. The first words of the First Amendment to our Constitution state: "Congress shall make no law respecting an establishment of religion, or prohibiting the free exercise thereof."[1] That means our government cannot make laws and policies that favor one religion over another. It also means it cannot favor being non-religious over being religious. While there are lengthy arguments about when an exception for a military necessity is within the bounds of the Constitution, simply stated, the government may not restrict the free exercise of religion.

The freedom of religion is guaranteed to the men and women serving in the military just like it is for every other American. That's the reason we have chaplains serving military members and their families wherever they are around the world. It's also why the practice of having government-paid chaplains for the military has withstood every challenge in the courts.

Did you know military chaplaincy predates the US Constitution? It's true. Government-funded military chaplains were already serving when our Constitution was approved on September 17, 1787. From the beginning of our country, it has been understood that since the military can send its members far away from their faith communities, ask them to risk their lives in the course of their duties, and require them to work in places and at times that restrict their ability to freely practice their faith, the government is obligated to provide for their religious needs. Chaplains are there to ensure members of the military enjoy the same religious freedom guaranteed in the Constitution for every American. So the chaplains' presence with military members is a constitutional obligation.

It's also personal.

I remember the day when the four-star chief of staff spoke to our Chaplain Corps leadership in Washington, DC. I'll never forget his words and the emotion in his voice as he concluded his talk that day with "Take care of my babies."[2]

That rather shocking statement from the highest-ranking officer in the Air Force resonated with every one of us in the room that day. We understood his use of such a tender word to describe those who served under his authority. The airmen were dear to us as well. We wore their uniform and worked alongside them. We ran PT—physical training—with them.[3] We deployed for months at a time with them. We cared for their families while they were deployed. We worshipped with them. We celebrated promotions, weddings, and new babies with them. We grieved with them and honored the memory of those who didn't come home. Every military chaplain worth his or her salt cares deeply for the men and women in uniform and their families. The feeling is genuine and heartfelt. It's far more than a paycheck. To be a chaplain is to fulfill a calling to give your life away for others.

No matter how deeply I cared, there was no way I—as just one chaplain—could have listened to and encouraged *every* airman going to war that year. Just like the airman who sat next to me, thousands would deploy and leave loved ones to fend for themselves for four to twelve months. And each one would have a story. However, I knew I could do something for *this* airman God had placed in the seat next to me. It's always a good idea to do for one what you wish you could do for all. I also had come to believe that God had appointments for me that weren't always penciled in on my calendar. God had called me and prepared me for this moment. This was ministry along the way.

A BRASS COIN

I wanted to give this worried young warrior something to take with him into his first combat experience as a reminder that a chaplain was in his corner and praying for him. You may know that senior officers and senior NCOs (noncommissioned officers) often carry a personal challenge coin to honor a deserving airman. Since I was a colonel and the command chaplain responsible for teams serving nearly a hundred thousand airmen at fifteen locations or more, my coin was emblazoned with the bright-red, blue, and yellow shield of Air Combat Command on one side and the seal of the Air Force Chaplain Corps on the other. I just happened to have one with me. I put the coin in my right palm and shook my traveling companion's hand. He lit up. Immediately he pulled his wallet from his back pocket, and there, tucked in with his military ID card for safe keeping, was another treasured coin similar to the one I had just given him.

With a coin in each hand now and grinning from ear to ear, he declared, "That makes two!"

I still smile thinking about that moment.

"How did you get your first coin?" I asked.

He gave me a name with the highest enlisted rank in the Air Force, chief master sergeant, in front of it. I asked him why the chief gave him his coin.

"I was Airman of the Year for the wing," he answered proudly.

For my nonmilitary friends, that's a really big deal.

Even with the affirmation of two challenge coins in your pocket, if you're one of the lowest-ranking people in a great big Air Force and you're given orders to go somewhere you wouldn't choose to go and leave someone you'd never leave at a time like this, you might come to a false conclusion. You might believe the lie that you're insignificant or your life doesn't matter as much as others. You may also get the mistaken idea that you're not important to God. You may think God is not hearing your prayers or he is against you.

SOLID-GOLD TRUTH

Challenge coins are great, but I wanted to give this airman something more than a promise to pray for him and a brass coin to carry in his pocket. I wanted to give him some solid-gold truth to carry in his heart. I knew this young man and his wife could both be heading into the toughest times of their young lives. He was concerned about what lay ahead of him. He was also worried about his wife giving birth to their first baby without him there. I can only imagine what was going through her heart and mind as she was going through her first pregnancy and facing childbirth without her husband.

I remembered what it felt like to be a thousand miles away when our first daughter was born. I also remembered my long night in the ICU and how God was with me even then. I knew God loved this young couple and their baby. I knew he wanted them to trust him through this hard time. And I was certain he wanted them to trust him even though nothing about this deployment and its timing felt right to them.

I pulled a Bible out of the well-traveled backpack at my feet. I opened it to a passage written by a lowly shepherd boy. This kid had one epic career path. God took him from herding sheep to leading a nation and becoming Israel's greatest king. Along the way, he also experienced the life of a warrior. He knew a thing or two about facing danger. He knew what it was like to be afraid. Once when he was captured by his enemy, he wrote a song: "When I am afraid, I put my trust in you. . . . In God I trust and am not afraid. What can mere mortals do to me?" (Psalm 56:3–4). He knew the pain of separation and loneliness. He had also grieved the loss of a child and felt the shame of personal failure. He had the kind of life experience that could speak with great credibility into this airman's life. I placed my open Bible in his hands and asked him to read the passage in front of him.

Who could say what God had in store for this young man sitting beside me? Who could say what titles he would wear during his lifetime? Whatever labels he might wear—airman, officer, husband, father, civilian leader—I knew he would need this encouragement. Regardless of the challenges he and his wife would face as their futures unfolded, there was a truth I wanted him to take with him on his journey: There is a God who loves you and your wife and your unborn baby, who hears your prayers, who is always watching over you, and who prepares people to come alongside you to help when life is hard.

The engines were droning, and the flight attendants were closing up the hatches. With each passing minute this flight would carry my young friend farther and farther from home and his sweet wife, who carried their first child, and ever closer to the danger of war. He read aloud the words that had become dear to me, the words of David—shepherd boy, warrior, poet, king, man after God's heart. Let's look at Psalm 121 once more:

> I lift up my eyes to the mountains—
>   where does my help come from?
> My help comes from the LORD,
>   the Maker of heaven and earth.
>
> He will not let your foot slip—
>   he who watches over you will not slumber;
> indeed, he who watches over Israel
>   will neither slumber nor sleep.
>
> The LORD watches over you—
>   the LORD is your shade at your right hand;
> the sun will not harm you by day,
>   nor the moon by night.
>
> The LORD will keep you from all harm—
>   he will watch over your life;
> the LORD will watch over your coming and going
>   both now and forevermore.

As soon as he finished reading the last line, he beamed and said, "Wow, I'm going to send that to my wife!"

What do you think? Good words for a young man heading into his first combat experience? Could this also be the truth his pregnant wife needed to know? There was a vast ocean between her and the support of her family, and she'd just sent her husband off to war. If she had ever dreamed of what marriage and her first pregnancy would be like, I'd venture to say this wasn't it.

Let me ask you: If you could sit with this young wife or her anxious husband for a moment, what's the truth you'd want them to know? If they trusted you enough to share the kind of spiritual desert that anxiety and fear can create, could you point them to an oasis?

For some, the gap between their expectations of life, with all their hopes and dreams, and the painful realities is so great they lose hope. In that arid place, they begin to believe the lie that no one can understand what they're going through, and no one can help.

PEYTON'S STORY

Be advised that this section includes a suicide story.

Peyton dreamed of being a Marine. It seemed clear to his family that he was born for the part. He was tall and strong and fearless, with the heart of a hero. He seemed to have an inner sense that when you're big and strong, your job is to defend those who are not. When he reached high school, he enrolled in his school's Marine Corps Junior ROTC program. The officer in charge saw Peyton's leadership ability and his never-waning passion to be a Marine. Each new school year, Peyton signed up for JROTC. Each year, he was promoted through the cadet ranks and given greater responsibility. In his senior year, he proudly pinned the insignia of *Cadet Commander* on his uniform shirt.

Finally, with four years of JROTC and high school graduation behind him, Peyton went to the Marine recruiter and started the process to enlist. When the time came, he went for his physical, certain he'd soon be a Marine. But there was bad news. A medical issue disqualified him. He was devastated.

He tried to come up with a plan B, but a series of disappointments followed, including a failed attempt at college and a breakup with his girlfriend. Peyton couldn't seem to regain his footing.

Without giving a clue to anyone, the day before his twentieth birthday, Peyton ended his life in his car, parked several miles from the house where he lived with his family. For his mother, the pain was excruciating, almost unbearable. It still is. His dad tried to be strong for his family, but often his grief overwhelmed him. It was crushing for Peyton's younger brothers and impossible for them to understand. Everyone was asking themselves, *What could I have done?* But there were no answers.

Imagine you had an opportunity to sit and listen to Peyton tell his story. What would you say to him or to others who've lost hope and bought into the lie that if some cherished dream doesn't happen, or the one you love chooses not to be with you, then life is not worth living? Maybe you are the one in a dark place right now, and you're the one searching for a reason to go on.

I asked Peyton's mom and dad if I could share his story with you. They hope it can help someone escape a downward spiral and find hope. Peyton's story reminds me how important it is to know the truth that we are loved more than we imagine, and life is worth living even when it doesn't turn out the way we planned.

I know what you're going through may be complicated, and I'm not writing to judge. I'm concerned you may have isolated yourself. You may be suffering deep depression alone. Family and friends may have no idea what's really going on in your life or how much you're hurting. Maybe someone has told you that you're drinking too much or that your drug use has become a problem. Maybe a relationship you were counting on has failed.

Maybe you're facing some overwhelming financial or legal issues. You may be struggling with physical or mental health challenges. Maybe hardest of all, even when you're surrounded by others, you may feel you're alone and without hope. If any of that describes where you are, please talk to someone now. God never intended for you to fight this battle alone.

Depression and emotional pain can dangerously warp your perception. You may see suicide as a way to make the pain stop. The truth is that it just transfers great pain to others to carry. I watched as Peyton's family suffered indescribable pain following his death. The agony of losing their son was unbearable for his mother and father. It's been several years now since Peyton took his life, and the pain goes on. The ache in their hearts will never end.

> **God never intended for you to fight this battle alone.**

The most difficult thing I ever did as a military chaplain was deliver a next-of-kin notification after a young airman took her life. We knocked on the door of her parents' home and waited. When her father opened the door and saw three of us there in our uniforms, he must have known what happened. Before anyone said a word, he collapsed onto the floor in anguish. He was hysterical with grief. I'd never witnessed such raw pain before.

Depression and pain can blind you to the truth that things can and do change. A person suffering in a fog of depression sometimes can't see the beautiful things standing right before them or the better days that are ahead. Would you trust me when I tell you there are things you may not be able to see right now that are true nonetheless? Just because you're unable to see the better days ahead doesn't mean they aren't real. One day a new friend will show up. A breakthrough will happen. An answer will come. A door will open. Circumstances will change.

The way you feel will change. I don't know how it will happen, but one day there will be joy on the other side of this present darkness. Morning will come.

IT WAS THERE ALL THE TIME

My first assignment as an active-duty chaplain was to Yokota Air Base, Japan. We arrived there on the Fourth of July. All through that summer, people told us about Mount Fuji. They told us how beautiful it is and how it stands in full view from the place where we lived. I couldn't see it at all. It was hard to believe it really was as near as they claimed. Finally fall arrived, and the first typhoon of the season blew in. Wind and heavy rain battered our little house in Mizuho, outside Tokyo, all through the night.

I awoke the next morning, dressed for work, and walked out the front door. The sky was shockingly blue. The air was clean and crisp. The cloud of gray smog that had hung over us ever since we arrived had been swept away by the storm. I slid into my car and headed to the base. I turned the corner in our neighborhood, and there it was! It seemed like Mount Fuji was standing at the end of our street, majestic and magnificent in its perfect symmetry. It had been there all the time, of course. I just couldn't see it—until now.

I have to tell you there may be some things you're thinking right now that just aren't so. You may believe the myth that if others really knew you, they wouldn't love you. The truth is that God knows you completely and loves you unconditionally. There's nothing you've ever said or done or thought that he doesn't already know. Here's the amazing truth: The One who knows you best is the One who loves you most!

Here's another truth for you: There are people who will listen without judgment. There are people who care and can help. Call someone. Better still, go talk to someone now. Find a chaplain. Talk to a pastor. Go see a medical or mental health provider. Confide in a family member. Text a friend. Do it now. You can be sure of this: God has prepared someone who can understand what you're going through, someone who will listen without judgment, someone who will care.

If you've thought about suicide, or you're worried about a friend or loved one, or you need some emotional support, there is a Lifeline network available 24/7 across the United States. It serves as a veterans' crisis line as well. Call this three-digit number now: 988. Someone will listen to you without judgment. They will take the time to understand how your problem is affecting you, provide support, and share resources that can help you. Your call is confidential and free. If you'd prefer to text rather than talk on the phone, you can also contact a trained crisis counselor and discuss any issue that's troubling you by texting HOME to 741741. This service is also free and available 24/7 in the United States.

I have a dream that someday every employee in America will have access to a chaplain—someone they know and trust, someone they can call when they're feeling hopeless, someone who is trained to help. Whether it's in the military or a civilian workplace, I know chaplains save lives. In the first six months of this year, in a company we serve with twenty-five thousand employees, chaplains intervened in seventeen situations where someone was thinking about taking their life.

MY STORY

You may think you're the first to travel the road you're on. But there is someone who has been where you are. In my second assignment as an active-duty chaplain, I became deeply depressed. I was in a dark place. I was pretty sure I knew why. I had a boss who seemed to go out of his way to make my life as difficult as possible. He seemed to find pleasure in humiliating me in front of others, and I hated that. I had never experienced anything like that before, and it appeared the stress was causing other problems for me. I would wake up in the morning feeling exhausted, dreading the drive to work. Several times when I was preaching a sermon I had labored over, without warning, my mind would go blank. I couldn't remember where I was going with a thought. It was more than embarrassing. Each time it happened, my stress amped up, and I became more depressed. I was on a downward spiral.

> **God has prepared someone who can understand what you're going through, someone who will listen without judgment, someone who will care.**

Then one day I knew I had to do something. I was driving home from work and suddenly realized I didn't recognize where I was. I backtracked until I saw something familiar and found my way home, where I finally talked to my wonderful Ruth about it. I should have opened up to her long before this.

I didn't know what to do or whom to call. I just knew I needed help. I was reluctant to see a medical or mental health doctor, fearing what that may do to my career. I was wrong about that. Let me repeat, *I was wrong about that!* I couldn't talk to the chaplain. I was the chaplain. So as I talked to my sweet wife, I prayed a silent prayer. *God, help me!*

Ruth said, "Why don't you talk to Chaplain Posey. I think that would be a good place to start."

I agreed and decided to give our retired chaplain friend a call. He picked me up at work the next day and took me to lunch at a restaurant off the base. I trusted him and knew our conversation would be confidential. I poured it all out—the anger, the depression, the exhaustion, the mental fog, and the dark, hopeless way I felt. Swallowing my pride and the need to present an "I've got it all together" image, I held nothing back. That day I experienced what it was like to be on the other side of the counseling equation. For the first time, I saw from the perspective of one seeking help and searching for hope, and saw the enormous value in that sacred space of confidentiality. After our lunch my chaplain friend prayed for me. I knew he had heard me and genuinely cared about me.

He called me the next day. "I happened to notice yesterday when we were talking at the restaurant that you have some white patches on your hands. Sometimes people who have those white patches of vitiligo, like you have, also have hypothyroidism. I think your symptoms fit that. I want you to get an appointment with a dermatologist at Wilford Hall Medical Center and ask them to check your thyroid."

Then he asked me, "Do you know how I know about the connection between hypothyroidism and vitiligo?"

"No, but I hope you're going to tell me," I said.

"My doctor told me about it years ago. You see, I have the same issue. Like you, I have the white patches of vitiligo on my skin, and I also have hypothyroidism."

I made the appointment just as Chaplain Posey suggested. At first the doctor wasn't interested in testing me for hypothyroidism. But before I left, for some reason he reversed course and agreed to order the blood work.

Several days later, I got a call from the doctor. "Chaplain Page, I need to apologize to you. I was reluctant to test you for this. We stopped screening people with vitiligo for hypothyroidism long ago because that association is rare. The fact is, you are hypothyroid, and on top of that you have no discernible levels of B12."

He went on. "That's the bad news. The good news is you're going to feel much better very soon."

And he was exactly right.

My chaplain friend who was there for me during that tough season in my life is now ninety-six years old, widowed, and in an assisted living facility in San Antonio. Ruth and I made a trip to see him several years ago. I wanted to thank him one more time and make sure he knew I would never forget what he had done for me.

Was it a coincidence that once I came to my senses and agreed to reach out for help, the next day the retired chaplain sitting across from me was perhaps the one-in-a-million person who could help? He had been through exactly what I was going through. He was *the* person who was able to connect me with the medical care I needed. That lunch with the chaplain changed my life.

I've shared this personal story with you just to give you a glimpse of hope and encourage you to talk to someone. I want you to see how God can work when you're willing to ask for help. Your situation is probably nothing like mine, but I guarantee you this: It is not unique. No matter what you're going through, someone somewhere has been where you are. The chances are good God has already brought somebody else through the storm you're in. I believe if you're willing, God will connect you to someone or to a group who can help. I believe God has prepared someone for such a time as this.

The crucial step in my getting better was deciding to ask for help. As I write these words, I'm praying for you. I'm asking God to help you muster the courage and the energy you need right now to reach out. I'm asking God to send you to a caring person who will hear your story with empathy and understanding, someone who will listen without judgment and connect you with the help you need. My prayer is that in your search for hope, you'll also find a team to join you in whatever battle you're facing.

For someone reading this, life has taken a turn you didn't see coming. Nothing is working out like you planned. Through circumstances beyond your control, you're heading into something you would never have chosen for yourself, and the timing couldn't be worse. Maybe you're the designated worrier for your family. Maybe your imagination is working overtime, thinking of what could happen. Maybe you are afraid and feeling inadequate for what might be ahead of you. If I could sit with you today and listen to your story, I would tell you, "Don't let your circumstances talk you out of what you know to be true. The truth is, you matter to God. He is for you. You don't have to walk this hard road alone. He has prepared someone who can help."

You can be sure God is for you because . . .

God has prepared someone who can provide the encouragement and help you need.

PRAYER

Father, there are times when I feel like nothing about my life is within my control. I confess I worry about what is ahead. Sometimes I question whether I'm equal to the task. I fret about the safety and well-being of the people I love. Lord, I know I have an alternative to fear. Today I choose to trust you with this situation. As I breathe in, fill me with me your peace. As I exhale, take away my anxious thoughts and calm my heart. Direct me to someone I can talk to without fear of judgment. I will listen for your voice in the encouraging words of those who care about me. Lord, please help me to not let pride or anger or fear keep me from getting the help I need. In Jesus's name I pray. Amen.

TALK IT OVER

1. Imagine that God has someone prepared to encourage and help you. How might you recognize them? What will you do now to connect with them?

2. Share a time when someone gave you the encouragement or help you needed. How did they encourage you? How did they help you?

3. Share a time when you were able to encourage someone because you had already experienced what they

were going through. How did you encourage them? How did you help them?

4. After reading this chapter, is there someone you're concerned about? What is your prayer for them? How will you reach out to them today? What would you say to someone who is thinking of suicide?

5. If you're a company leader, how could chaplains make a difference for your employees and for your business?

A SONG TO LIFT YOUR SPIRIT

"I Need a Miracle" by Third Day

Chapter 4

NIGHT VISION GOGGLES

When you pass through the waters, I will be with you; and when you pass through the rivers, they will not sweep over you. When you walk through the fire, you will not be burned; the flames will not set you ablaze.

Isaiah 43:2

Have I not commanded you? Be strong and courageous. Do not be afraid; do not be discouraged, for the LORD your God will be with you wherever you go.

Joshua 1:9

I was twelve years old when the Beatles made their first appearance in the United States on *The Ed Sullivan Show*. It was Sunday night, February 9, 1964. If you were alive in '55, chances are you were watching TV that night. But I missed it. I wasn't one of the seventy-four million people who tuned in to see the Beatles and shattered TV audience records, but I clearly remember it was all the buzz the next day at school. A week later someone came up with the brilliant idea to hold a mock election and let the middle school students answer the burning question of the day: Who's more popular, Elvis or the Beatles? It was a tight race, but I think the Fab Four edged out the King of Rock and Roll that day.

That was 1964. What if we go back several years before my childhood to 1000 BC? What singer-songwriter was creating all the buzz in those days? The answer has to be the artist formerly known as David. The guitar of that day was the ten-stringed lyre, and the handsome young David could make it talk. In fact, it was his reputation as a talented lyre player that landed him a gig playing his music for Israel's first king (1 Samuel 16:17–23).

From that promising start, David would go on to become a towering figure in music history. His influence spans not just decades but three millennia. He's revered in Judaism, Christianity, and Islam for his heart for God and the songs he wrote, which span almost every emotion. We can still see his impact on popular music and the worship of billions of people even to this day. Regardless of the worship style, if you check the lyrics we sing in church or synagogue even now, you'll find words from David's pen and see evidence of his influence. Look through Psalms and you'll discover 73 of those 150 sacred songs are attributed to David,[1] though he surely wrote many more than that. According to an ancient document found in Qumran near the Dead Sea, he wrote more than four thousand.[2] Of all the songs David wrote, however, if there is one that stands out as his greatest hit, it has to be the one that begins with the words "The Lord is my shepherd" and includes this famous line you've probably heard before: "Even though I walk through the valley of the shadow of death, I will fear no evil, for you are with me" (Psalm 23:4 ESV).

This song has been top of the charts for three thousand years. Its ability to speak to people in vastly different times and places must have something to do with the fact that sooner or later, we all find ourselves in a dark valley. It's a universal human experience. At some point you and I will walk a path not of our choosing, full of dark shadows.

> **Sooner or later, we all find ourselves in a dark valley. It's a universal human experience.**

Toward the end of his long life, David looked back and remembered such a dark valley. From his days as a shepherd boy, he also recalled pleasant green pastures and refreshing pools of quiet water. In the creative mind of the poet, the peaceful ponds, the verdant grasslands, and even the fearsome valley with its chilling shadows all became pictures of moments in his life.

His point was that in each of those settings—representing the good times and the hard times—David was there with a Shepherd. It was the Shepherd who led him to the life-giving places that sustained him and restored his strength. It was the Shepherd's presence that calmed his fear in the hard places. To David, the Lord was not just *a* shepherd. He was bold enough to call him *my* Shepherd. It was his relationship with the Lord, the Shepherd of his life, that made all the difference.

David was eminently qualified to write this song. He knew a thing or two about being a shepherd. He knew how dependent sheep are on their shepherds for daily life. He also knew how defenseless they are when attacked by a predator. Having a good shepherd was not only the key to a good life but their only hope of staying alive.

David knew something that would be good for you and me to know too: The quality of a sheep's life is totally dependent on the one who stands at the head of the flock and calls them by name to follow him. He knew their security is directly related to who their shepherd is. He knew that was also true for him and everyone else.

We still love David's song of the Shepherd three thousand years after he wrote it. Many have a story of how his words comforted them in the loss of a loved one or strengthened them on a hard day. Through the ages, David's words have provided millions of wounded souls the glimpses of hope they needed. I want to tell you the story of how the essential truth David shares in Psalm 23 helped a young lieutenant from Texas survive the abuse of his captors and remain unbroken.

VIEW FROM A PRISON CAMP

Robert Preston Taylor signed up to serve as a chaplain in the Army Air Corps, and soon after, in May 1941, he deployed to the Philippines.[3] On December 7, the Japanese attacked Pearl Harbor, Hawaii. Ten hours later they launched an assault on the Philippines.

After four harrowing months of ferocious combat, the unthinkable happened. On April 9 at 9:00 a.m., white flags went up, signaling the surrender of American forces in the Philippines. Chaplain Taylor was among nearly twelve thousand Americans taken prisoner. The brutal Bataan Death March began the next day. Estimates vary widely as to how many POWs died. Conservatively, several thousand Americans and Filipino allies succumbed to the heat and lack of food and water. Chaplain Taylor survived and was eventually transported to the Cabanatuan POW camp.

Taylor was among several chaplains at the camp who set about serving their fellow POWs. When he saw some of them suffering and dying due to lack of medication, he found a way to smuggle medicine into the camp. When his captors discovered the operation, Chaplain Taylor was caged in a bamboo heat box just four feet high and five feet long and left to die a slow, agonizing death in the blazing Philippine sun.

The chaplain wasn't alone in that box. He shared the painfully cramped space with a young private. Benny was only twenty years old, just a boy really, but he looked middle-aged from the deprivations of the POW camp. For weeks the two men suffered together in the sweltering heat and humidity with little food or water. Swarms of mosquitoes found their exposed flesh and added to their torment.

I've often wondered whether Chaplain Taylor's presence with Benny in the heat box could have been an answer to Benny's mother's agonizing prayer for her son. As a chaplain, I've had the distinct impression at times that I was standing in for a mom or dad who couldn't be there—a parent who was on their knees, pouring out their heart to God, and who would be there with a wounded, wayward, or struggling son or daughter if they could. Sometimes when you're wondering, *Why am I here? Why am I going through this?* look around you and see if there's someone who needs your help. That just might be the day you show up as the answer to somebody's prayer.

Once when Benny panicked seeing the guards coming toward them, Chaplain Taylor tried to bolster his young friend. "Our lives are in God's hands, Benny."

"What God?" Benny shot back at him. "I haven't seen him around here lately!"

One day after they were forced to witness the execution of four officers who had attempted an escape, the guards escorted them back to the heat boxes. As night fell, the mosquitoes returned with a vengeance. In the darkness, Chaplain Taylor turned toward Benny to comfort him with words that had become precious to him: David's Twenty-Third Psalm.

> The LORD is my shepherd; I shall not want.
>   He makes me lie down in green pastures.
> He leads me beside still waters.
>   He restores my soul.
> He leads me in paths of righteousness
>   for his name's sake.

Even though I walk through the valley of the
shadow of death,
I will fear no evil,
for you are with me;
your rod and your staff,
they comfort me.

You prepare a table before me
in the presence of my enemies;
you anoint my head with oil;
my cup overflows.
Surely goodness and mercy shall follow me
all the days of my life,
and I shall dwell in the house of the LORD
forever.[4]

Benny listened intently then responded, with a voice barely audible, "My mom taught me that when I was a kid. I'd sure like to believe it, Chaplain Taylor. If only it were real."

"It's real, Benny," he assured him. "It's real!"

Benny drifted into a deep sleep for the first time in days. The next morning dawned as the days before had, with no food or water. Then at midday a guard appeared and carefully measured out a small portion of rice to Benny and Chaplain Taylor. While the food, water, and sleep boosted Benny's morale, it was the chaplain's words the day before that had restored his hope.

"Chaplain, that Bible reading last night touched me down here," Benny said, pointing to his heart.

Taylor responded by putting his Bible in Benny's hands. "You can read it anytime you wish."

One by one, as the men in the heat boxes succumbed to disease and deprivation, the burial squad was ordered to take them away. Chaplain Taylor wondered whether he'd be next. After fourteen weeks, he was no longer able to digest the small bit of rice that was keeping him alive, and he vomited everything he tried to eat. By evening, a helpless and emaciated Chaplain

Taylor lay pale and motionless in his cell. Someone reported to one of the colonels that Taylor was dead. Like the others who had died in the heat boxes, they would bury him unceremoniously in a grave his fellow prisoners would dig. But the burial didn't happen. When the guard allowed the colonel to go to Taylor, he found him lifeless just as he had heard. He put an ear to Chaplain Taylor's chest. He detected a faint heartbeat. He was still clinging to life. The guard allowed the men to take him to Zero Ward to die.

When word got around the camp that Chaplain Taylor needed their prayers, the prisoners organized a prayer effort that went on day and night for two weeks. Survival seemed unlikely. Whenever he was conscious, Chaplain Taylor suffered delirium, thinking he was still in the heat box. Undeterred, the men of the camp continued to pray for a miracle.

One month went by, then two. Then, against all odds, the day came when Chaplain Taylor was able to walk out of Zero Ward leaning on a bamboo stick, weak but very much alive. Practically a living skeleton, but unbroken, Chaplain Taylor encouraged the men to never give up hope. The men gathered around him, buoyed by the fact they were witnessing a miracle. For many, their faith was strengthened that day, and some came to put their trust in Jesus for the first time. The chaplain had become a symbol of hope for them. They saw him as a living answer to prayer.

Each time I tell this story, inevitably someone will ask, "What happened to Benny?" I wish I could tell you. All my searching has not turned up any information on him. What I do know about Benny is this: When life was hard, God sent a chaplain to be with him. In his suffering, he was not alone. Someone was there to remind him of a mother and a God who loved him dearly.

President Robert Sloan Jr. of Baylor University honored Chaplain Taylor posthumously in 2004, presenting the inaugural Chaplain Robert P. Taylor Award for Baylor War Heroes to Chaplain Taylor's widow, Millie Taylor, and their son, Bob. Robert Sloan called Chaplain Taylor "the most notable example of sustained heroism among military chaplains."[5] Chaplain Major General Lorraine Potter also spoke at the ceremony that day. She quoted Chaplain Taylor's own words. They were the words he spoke to the men who witnessed the miracle of his survival: "If you turn me inside out and look in my heart, you would see a man who still believes in the power of God."[6]

> **In his suffering, Benny was not alone. Someone was there to remind him of a mother and a God who loved him dearly.**

In an interview, Chaplain Taylor shared several things that kept him alive through forty-two months of imprisonment. He had realized it was not all about him. He wasn't staying alive just for himself—he needed to be strong for others. As a chaplain he stayed busy caring for his fellow POWs. He credited his survival in part to that fact. Most of all, though, he said it was his faith in God that sustained him.[7]

There was another factor in his survival. The image of his beautiful wife Ione and the reunion that awaited them gave him reason to survive. Whatever happened, he simply would not give up on the day he would hold her in his arms again.

Finally the day arrived he had dreamed of for so long. When he disembarked in San Francisco, Ione was there waiting. She was as lovely as the day he'd kissed her goodbye when he left for the Philippines. He reached out to embrace her.

She pulled back from him. Nothing could have prepared him for what she said next. "I remarried just a month ago. Preston, they told me you were dead."

Sometime later, Chaplain Taylor revealed his thoughts in that moment. "At first, I felt alone. I wondered if God had deserted me. But then the doubt passed. I remembered how the Lord had been with me through it all. I knew he was with me now."[8]

Years later Robert Preston Taylor was nominated by President John F. Kennedy and confirmed by the Senate to be the third Air Force chief of chaplains. It was a humbling thing for me to sit at the desk of this hero during my Pentagon assignment as the twenty-fourth deputy chief of chaplains.

A framed official photo of Chaplain Taylor, a gift from our daughters for my promotion to brigadier general, hung on the wall of my Pentagon office. Today it graces the room where I'm writing this. Anne and Allison placed a quote from Chaplain Taylor at the bottom of the photo. It's been the solid-gold truth I've carried in my heart through some difficult days. My prayer is that you'll take it with you, remember it on your difficult day, and hold on to your faith: "Never doubt in the darkness what you believed in the light."

A SURPRISING CHOICE OF SONGS

Chaplain Taylor and Benny were mistreated, abused, and tormented. They were suffering extreme deprivation. Their lives were hanging by a thread. To be honest, if I were in that situation, I'm not sure I would have identified so much with Psalm 23. I think the psalm before it would have come to mind. That psalm is sometimes called the Psalm of the Cross. The words sound like they must be the lament of Jesus suffering crucifixion, but they were actually written a thousand years before he died on the cross. Stripped of his clothes, nails piercing his hands and feet, hanging in agony from one of the cruelest tools of execution ever devised, Jesus cried out the opening words from David's song, directing us to those ancient words. "My God, my God, why have you forsaken me?" (Psalm 22:1). His words from the cross help us see that it's okay to tell God when we're feeling abandoned and wondering where God is in our suffering. In fact, Jesus's words remind us that asking God an honest question is far better than "babbling" on with many words that mean nothing to us (Matthew 6:7).

As I read David's song again today, I wonder when Jesus first identified with the words of Psalm 22. Did they occur to him suddenly as he suffered on the cross? I think not. Did the Holy Spirit use these words to reveal to young Jesus what manner of death he would die? (See also Isaiah 53.) Perhaps. While we may never know when he realized how closely those words describe his own agony on the cross, what we do know is that sometime in his life, he committed those words to memory. He had hidden them in his heart. Then on the hardest day of his life, they poured from his heart as a lament to God and gave honest voice to what he was feeling. In the same way, Bible verses we have memorized help us pray and give voice to what our hearts want to say to God when we're hurting.

I believe the words of Psalm 22 were more than a lament. I believe they were also written about the death Jesus would die, the purpose he had come to fulfill.

> My mouth is dried up like a potsherd,
> and my tongue sticks to the roof of my mouth;
> you lay me in the dust of death.
>
> Dogs surround me,
> a pack of villains encircles me;
> they pierce my hands and my feet.
> All my bones are on display;
> people stare and gloat over me.
> They divide my clothes among them
> and cast lots for my garment.
>
> (Psalm 22:15–18)

But Chaplain Taylor didn't share those words of Psalm 22 with Benny, even though to any observer they would have fit their situation. Rather, he turned to Psalm 23. Instead of questioning why God had forsaken him, he reminded himself of the Lord's presence with him in his suffering. "The LORD is my shepherd. . . . Even though I walk through the valley of the shadow of death, I will fear no evil, *for you are with me*" (vv. 1, 4 ESV).

What made the difference? Why Psalm 23 instead of Psalm 22? I believe it is the word *my* that made all the difference for Chaplain Taylor. Jesus was not just the Good Shepherd. Chaplain Taylor could say he was "my shepherd." Years before, he had chosen to make Jesus his Shepherd and follow him. He had been following him to green pastures and still waters long before he walked into this valley of dark shadows with him. And that made all the difference.

A theologian might explain that because Jesus suffered on the cross in our place, we will never have to experience separation from God. He paid in full the penalty for all our sin and canceled the debt we could never repay. Here's what's so amazing: He offers that to us as a gift! There is no condemnation and no separation from God for those who receive his gift.

Even so, how is it possible Chaplain Taylor could see the Lord was with him and Benny in such a dark place? How can you and I see that reality when the light has gone out in our world? An experience I had while trying out some impressive military equipment helped me to see there's such a thing in our spiritual lives for times like these.

BELIEVING IS SEEING

While I was stationed in San Antonio, Texas, I was invited to test out a pair of night vision goggles (NVGs) like our combat warriors use. I showed up at the appointed time, and the sergeant led me to a windowless room with tiered seating. After I took a seat on the top row, the lights went out. The room was completely dark. Although I could hear the sergeant's voice, I seemed to be alone in the room. If he had remained silent, you could have convinced me I was in the room by myself. Then I put the NVGs on and looked in the direction of his voice. There was a green-tinged man! Beyond any doubt, I could see the sergeant was standing in the room with me. I was amazed by this piece of technology, and I'll always be grateful to the great airman who invited his chaplain to experience this wonder.

It seems to me that Chaplain Taylor's faith was working just like night vision goggles. Even on his darkest night, where there seemed to be no light, he could see the Lord was with him. Even when he was mistreated, he could say with unshakable confidence, "I am not alone. The Lord is with me. I will trust him and not be afraid."

Even when he lost the future he had hoped for with his wife Ione, he didn't surrender to despair. He continued to trust a loving Father who would bring him through the darkness into the light of day again. And God did just that when he brought the lovely Millie Goode Taylor into his life.

I had the privilege to meet Chaplain Taylor's wife, Millie, their son, Bob, and Bob's family at an event in Washington, DC, in 2005. Millie brought several of her beloved husband's handwritten sermons with her. They were on scraps of paper that looked like he had rescued them from a recycle bin. She said it was always his habit never to waste paper. Although his handwritten notes were precious to her, she generously gave them—along with the rack of ribbons from Chaplain Taylor's uniform that bore witness to his many military honors and his service wheel cap—to be placed in a display case in the Chaplain Robert Preston Taylor Conference Room. It was a small honor for one who sacrificed so much for his country and gave us a worthy example of faith and faithfulness through unimaginable suffering.

After his years as a POW, Chaplain Taylor lived another fifty years and saw his grandchildren. But what if he had died in the heat box? He knew that even if his body failed, he would be with the Lord forever. Psalm 23 closes with words of sweet assurance: "I shall dwell in the house of the LORD forever" (v. 6 ESV).

Charles Spurgeon, the great English preacher, said, "While I am here I will be a child alone with my God; the whole world shall be His house to me; and when I ascend to the upper chamber, I shall not change my company, nor even change the house. I shall go to dwell in the upper story of the house of the Lord forever."[9]

Jesus talked about the house of the Lord: "My Father's house has many rooms; if that were not so, would I have told you that I am going there to prepare a place for you? And if I go and prepare a place for you, I will come back and take you to be with me that you also may be where I am" (John 14:2–3).

Psalm 23 doesn't promise we'll never walk through dark valleys. In fact, it assumes we will. It does promise, however, that even in life's darkest hour, we're not alone. What if your faith could see through the darkness you're going through now? What if you knew the Lord was with you with "grace sufficient" to meet every need and mercy to cleanse every stain?[10] What if you could see in the darkness that your Shepherd is still there before you, leading the way—the same One who has guided you, provided for you, and protected you in days past? I believe if you could see that, you could be strong and take the next step knowing this present darkness will not last forever. Morning will surely come.

You can be sure God is for you because . . .

God is with you in your darkest hour.

PRAYER

Lord, in my darkest hour, I am not alone. I know you are with me. I am holding on to the truth that you will not abandon me in my suffering. I choose to trust you in this darkness, until you bring me into the light of freedom and joy again. In Jesus's name I pray. Amen.

TALK IT OVER

1. Sheep depend on their shepherds to lead, provide, protect, and care for them. When has God been like a shepherd to you?

2. If your faith was working like night vision goggles right now, what truth would you be able to see? How would that change things in your life?

3. The truth of Psalm 23 helped Chaplain Taylor when he faced almost certain death. What Bible passage has helped you in a tough time?

4. What truth would you share with someone who feels like they're going through the darkest time of their life?

SONGS TO LIFT YOUR SPIRIT

"Psalm 23 (Surely Goodness, Surely Mercy)" by Shane & Shane

"Still Waters (Psalm 23)" by Leanna Crawford

Chapter 5

ALL US SPARROWS

She gave this name to the LORD who spoke to her: "You are the God who sees me," for she said, "I have now seen the One who sees me."

Hagar, when she was pregnant and alone (Genesis 16:13)

I had completed my first year of college as an aspiring music major when I was invited to sing with the amazing, one-of-a-kind Ethel Waters. You may not know that name, but in her day, just about everybody in America knew and loved Ethel Waters. She was a genuine superstar who deserves to be remembered not just for her talent and what she achieved but for what she overcame.

Ethel's mother was just twelve or thirteen when she conceived Ethel, the result of a rape by a much older family acquaintance. Growing up, Ethel was passed from relative to relative. The longest she lived in one place was fifteen months, and that was in a three-room shanty in the heart of the red-light district in Philadelphia, though she often slept over a warm iron grating on the street.[1] "I was never a child. I never was coddled, or liked, or understood by my family," Ethel said. "I was always an outsider."[2]

She was married to a man almost twice her age when she was just thirteen years old. After a year of abuse, she left him and got a job working as a maid for less than five dollars a week.[3] I suspect absolutely no one looked at this girl and imagined she would become a beloved Broadway, motion picture, and recording star. How could they have known she would be the first African American to star in her own nationwide TV show and the second to be nominated for an Academy Award?[4]

In October 1970, in LSU's Tiger Stadium, Ethel and I sang our hearts out to more than thirty thousand people who had come to Baton Rouge from across Louisiana and Mississippi to hear Billy Graham.

Before you get the wrong idea, I suppose I should tell you my singing with Ethel wasn't exactly a duet—or a trio. It wasn't even a quartet. Okay, Ethel may not have been aware I was singing with her. I was standing in the back left corner of a thirty-five-hundred-voice choir led by Billy Graham's music leader, Cliff Barrows. Would you like to hear it just like I heard it that night? Google "'His Eye Is on the Sparrow' by Ethel Waters." Many have recorded their version of this classic, but no one sings it quite like Ethel.

> Why should I feel discouraged?
> Why should the shadows come?
> Why should my heart be lonely
> And long for heav'n and home,
> When Jesus is my portion?
> My constant Friend is He:
> His eye is on the sparrow,
> And I know He watches me.[5]

Do you want to know why Ethel chose to sing that particular song for us in Tiger Stadium? Maybe it was because she had wowed audiences when she sang it on Broadway in 1950. She received a Best Actress award that year for her performance. Two years later, starring in a movie, she stole the show singing that same song without any musical accompaniment as she cradled a child on each side. When she published her autobiography in 1951, she titled it *His Eye Is on the Sparrow*.[6] It was a best seller. But I believe there was another reason she chose to sing that song for us. Although she didn't write the lyrics herself, you could say "His Eye Is on the Sparrow" was her song. In fact, Ethel's life story was summed up in those six words on her gravestone:

Ethel Waters
"His Eye Is on the Sparrow"
1896–1977[7]

Despite Ethel's success and the fame that came with it, she knew great sorrow and loneliness. She had suffered neglect, cruel injustice, and the consequences of poor choices. By 1957, when she walked into a Billy Graham crusade in Madison Square Garden, she was a "disillusioned, lonely, 61-year-old woman. . . . Ethel knew she was in debt to God and needed peace and reconciliation with him."[8] Here's how Ethel told the story of that night in her own words. "In 1957 . . . I, Ethel Waters, a 380-pound decrepit old lady, rededicated [my] life to Jesus Christ, and boy, because he lives, just look at me now. . . . I thank God for the privilege, eighteen years later, to still be able to say . . . his eye is still on all us sparrows."[9]

WHEN YOU WANT TO FLY AWAY

Let's revisit Psalm 121 for a moment. Remember how David announced, in his hour of need, "My help comes from the LORD, the Maker of heaven and earth" (v. 2). Then he reminded us of this great truth: The same God who was the source of his help is watching over you and me. This is David's life song about God's continuous loving care. He was celebrating the same truth that Ethel Waters came to treasure more than wealth or fame. We don't know the circumstances that moved David to write his song. When I read it, I can't help but imagine David, the warrior, writing from a deployment tent surrounded by enemy forces poised in the darkness, ready to strike at first light. Whatever the situation, he must have been desperate, because the thought of running to the hills for refuge crossed David's mind. "I lift up my eyes to the mountains—where does my help come from?" (v. 1). I can understand that. Maybe you've been there too.

While he may have written these words going through a crisis of his own, it seems David also intended them as a help for pilgrims on their way to the Holy City, Jerusalem.[10] They would travel several days from the hill country and distant plains to fulfill their obligation to worship in Jerusalem. With no chicken nuggets available in a drive-through to satisfy the car seat crew and not a hotel bed in sight as night fell, those travelers would be loaded down with all the provisions they needed for a days-long journey.

I can identify. My sweet wife loves to celebrate her July birthday with a family trip. Last year there were nine of us, including the three littles, the youngest of our five grandchildren. With two cars and a pickup all loaded to the max, you'd never know our beach destination was just an hour away and we were only staying three nights. Even with all the traveling we've done, Ruth and I have never quite mastered the art of traveling light. Can you picture us among the ancient pilgrims on our way to Jerusalem? I'd be leading a sad-eyed donkey piled high with clothes, tents, food, games, toys, an ice cream maker, a wok, and a Yeti the size of your grandfather's Buick. At least that's what we had going to the beach, but I digress.

David knew each traveler he was writing these words to would also be carrying an unseen burden. Just like for you and me, the heaviest loads were not the tent, or the food, or the other provisions. The heaviest loads were the ones no one could see.

Their stories were the same as ours. For some, life had been a series of failures and setbacks. Others carried deep wounds because someone had been unfair or even cruel. Some were grieving the loss of a loved one. Others carried the heavy weight of a secret shame. Trudging along, they would make their way on the uphill road to Jerusalem. Finally, approaching their destination, the sacred hills that surrounded the Holy City would come into view. The weary travelers would lift their eyes from the rough road beneath their feet to the beaconing mountains offering refuge. Perhaps, once on the hilltop and gazing down on Jerusalem, they would feel the presence of God.

I wonder whether you're making the journey with the weight of the world on your shoulders right now. Like David, maybe you long to leave the hard road and fly away to some hilltop hideaway, some place of refuge, and escape the pain and worries that ruin your days and rob you of sleep. Maybe the silent cry of your heart is, *Where does my help come from? Does anyone see me? Can anyone help?*

Isn't that the question all of us ask at some point in our lives? Live long enough and you're going to face a problem you can't solve with a YouTube video. So when that day comes—and it will come—who do you call?

Who do you call when the disease is incurable, your loss irreplaceable, and tomorrow seems impossible?

Who do you call when the hurt's unforgivable, the dark stain's indelible, and your shame feels unbearable?

Who do you call on a day like that? Where do you go or what do you do to escape pain, grief, or shame? Have you discovered that wherever you go, wherever your happy place may be, the problem somehow follows you there? Whatever you do, as soon as the distraction is gone, the anguish, the addiction, or the anger is still with you.

The good news is that David didn't run for refuge. He didn't head for the hills to escape his problem. Instead, he lifted his eyes above the hills to the One who made the hills. And he's invited you and me to do the same. When the heat's on, don't go with your first instinct and run for the nearest exit from the battle. Instead, lift your eyes to the God who sees you and fights for you.

In your hour of need, when the Enemy whispers that you don't matter, no one sees you, and you're on your own, don't believe it! Don't listen to the voice that says the only thing standing between you and disaster is *you*. The Enemy would have you believe that all you've got is *your* strength, *your* smarts, *your* resources, or *your* ability to get you through. And maybe you're feeling like none of those is your strong suit right now. Regardless of where you've been or what you're going through, the truth of Jesus's words that inspired Ethel's gospel anthem and the truth of David's psalm is clear: God sees you, and you are precious to him. Your need may be great, but it's no match for the unfailing love and power of God. Don't let fear or discouragement keep you cowering in a corner. Trust God even though your heart may be crushed.

> **David lifted his eyes above the hills to the One who made the hills. And he's invited you and me to do the same.**

Imagine this: The One who sees you and cares about you is none other than the One who spoke all that we see and all that we cannot see into existence. Is there anything too hard for the Maker of heaven and earth? Whatever his painful circumstance, David chose to trust the God who had helped him in times past. With the truth firmly fixed in his heart, he could say with confidence, "My help comes from the Lord, the Maker of heaven and earth" (Psalm 121:2). And so can you!

AUDACIOUS FAITH

That's a bit audacious, you say? Thinking the creator of the universe has the time or interest to focus his attention on one person out of the eight billion living on Planet Earth sounds far-fetched to you? *I'm no king like David,* you might say. *I'm not that spiritual and not nearly righteous enough. I'm no saint, just someone muddling through the best I can. If there's a God, why should he listen to me?*

Maybe the greatest myth-busting truth I've encountered in my life is this: God values the ordinary, the broken, the wounded, the weak, the wayward, the needy, the poor, the marginalized, the outcast, and the . . . well, you put your category in there. The ones society overlooks or casts aside are the very ones God loves. They're the ones he invites to walk with him. It's a consistent message from the Bible.

> Whoever oppresses the poor shows contempt for
> their Maker,
> but whoever is kind to the needy honors God.
> (Proverbs 14:31)

> Learn to do right; seek justice.
> Defend the oppressed.
> Take up the cause of the fatherless;
> plead the case of the widow.
> (Isaiah 1:17)

> The King will say . . . "I was hungry and you gave me something to eat, I was thirsty and you gave me something to drink, I was a stranger and you invited me in, I needed clothes and you clothed me . . . I was in prison and you came to visit me. . . .
>
> ". . . Truly I tell you, whatever you did for one of the least of these brothers and sisters of mine, you did for me." (Matthew 25:34–36, 40)

Manuel Scott was the son of a sharecropper growing up near Waco, Texas, in the 1930s.[11] One day, young Manuel thought of the tasty cookies that were baked at the little mom-and-pop store near where he lived. After they cooled, the cookies were bagged and sold at a price Manuel could only dream of holding in his hand, but he knew a few of the broken cookies would be bagged together and sold for a penny. On this day he yearned for one of those bags of broken cookies—but he didn't have a penny.

A woman in the community had taken an interest in Manuel and invited him to go to church with her. One day she told him, "Manuel, Jesus loves you." Well, it seems little Manuel must have taken that message to heart. Not only did he believe Jesus loved him but, as he said it, "I had the *audacity* to believe the God of the universe saw me and cared about me. I believed he had an *individualized concern* for me."

So I ask you, what would you do if you knew God had an individualized concern for you? Well, I'll tell you what Manuel did. He headed to the store. And as he walked, he prayed. And as he prayed, he walked. I like that approach to prayer. Like so many other things in my life, writing the book you hold in your hands has been a "pray as I walk and walk as I pray" experience. I wonder what might happen in your life if you were to pray, trust God, and take the next step? So what do you think happened as young Manuel walked the roadside to the store that day?

> **What would you do if you knew God had an individualized concern for you?**

Come on now—does the Creator really hear a barefoot boy's prayer as he walks along some backwater roadside in Texas looking for a penny? Better yet, does the Maker of heaven and earth even care that some kid in Waco has his heart set on a bag of broken cookies? Let's keep going. Does God care that you were passed over for promotion? Does God care that you've been betrayed by the one who made a promise to you? Does God care that your heart's desire is to hold a baby? Does God care that you're sick or lonely or out of work? I'll let you decide. But

I know how Manuel Scott would answer those questions. He shouted with a hand in the air, "I found a penny!"

A FRIEND'S SURPRISING SUPERPOWER

I've always been interested in learning how well-known songs came to be. Sometimes you'll find a great story behind the lyrics that makes the search worthwhile. For example, I recently discovered what inspired one of the greatest rock songs of all time. It happened during a phone call keyboardist Jonathan Cain made to his dad. Jonathan had moved to LA with a dream of making it big in the music world. Discouraged, he called his dad to ask him for another loan. During their conversation, he asked, "Dad, should I just give up on this thing and come home?"

His dad's answer became the hook for one of the best-selling digital tracks in the twentieth century, which would rack up over a billion plays on Spotify.[12] He said, "No, no, don't come home. Stick to your guns. Don't stop believin'!"[13] I guess you've figured out I'm talking about Journey's 1981 megahit "Don't Stop Believin'."

After reading that story, I was curious to know how "His Eye Is on the Sparrow" came to be. I wondered whether there might be a story there.

I discovered the words to this beloved gospel song came from the pen of a music teacher from Nova Scotia named Civilla Martin. According to the hymn writer herself, the inspiration for the song came when she and her husband traveled to Elmira, New York, to visit Civilla's dear friend and her husband. Civilla's friend had been bedridden for almost twenty years, and her husband also had a seriously limiting disability. Each morning he would say goodbye to his wife and leave in his wheelchair for work.

Here were two people who could have been bitter about how life had turned out for them, and yet they were happy. How is it possible their friends were so joyful despite their situation? Well, that's exactly what Civilla's husband wanted to know. So he asked this cheerful couple for the secret to their "bright hopefulness."

Civilla's friend answered for the couple. "His eye is on the sparrow, and I know he watches me."[14] Don't misunderstand. It was not her friend's *disability* that inspired the gospel song known and loved by so many. It was her *ability* to live a life of joyful faith in spite of her circumstances. If Civilla's friend had a superpower, it was this: She was able to trust God with her disability and live a life of bright hopefulness. It was that triumphant faith that inspired the beloved gospel song recorded by Ethel Waters, Mahalia Jackson, Gladys Knight, Whitney Houston, Barbara Mandrell, Kirk Franklin, and many others.[15]

BIRDS WITH SOMETHING TO SAY

Our daughter Allison first learned to ride a bike when we lived in Mizuho, a neighborhood a short drive from the air base and about twenty miles from the heart of Tokyo. Our Japanese neighbors were warm and welcoming. We soon made friends with the Suganuma family and several others with kids about the same age as our seven-year-old Allie.

One day I turned onto our street to discover Allie's blond hair flying as she pedaled furiously, weaving down the narrow street with two little Japanese boys chasing after her, their faces beaming. As they ran, they were shouting something to her. I'm sure it must have translated roughly, "You're doing great! Keep pedaling!" Unfazed by the language barrier, Hisayuki and Takayuki had taught our Allie to ride a bicycle without the training wheels. It's one of my most cherished memories of our four years in Japan.

Eight months after we moved to the rented house in Mizuho, an apartment on the air base became available. We said goodbye to our Japanese friends and moved into base housing near the elementary school where Allie would be a second grader. One fine Saturday, as she and I rode our bicycles, two birds sat unafraid in the grass at the edge of the sidewalk, watching us like spectators at a NASCAR race. Their little heads turned in sync as we pedaled past them. We both laughed about how the birds were out people-watching that day.

Since those days I've become a bird-watcher. I don't know how this happens, but it seems to me you turn sixty and suddenly this strange and inexplicable need to know the names of birds hits you. And just like that, it happened to us. Ruth and I have become fascinated with the birds in our neighborhood. Scissor-tailed flycatchers are great fun to watch. They ignore us as they dart and dive, performing fantastic air shows over our backyard like they're Air Force Thunderbirds. Whistling-ducks, oblivious to us following them with our upturned faces, fly overhead in kind of a messy V, all screeching noisily at the same time as if they have different opinions on which way to go. They're our favorite. The great blue heron that stands regal and silent at the water's edge is different though. He keeps a cautious eye on us as we approach. When we pass behind him, he twists his head around to watch us with his other eye.

Jesus said there was something life-changing we can learn from watching birds. It happened one day when he sat down in the grass on a hillside that formed a natural amphitheater, and the crowd sat in tiers above him. He had much to teach them that would challenge almost every notion of what they thought was true. He did some serious myth busting. Again and again Jesus repeated the hook, "You have heard. . . . But I tell you . . ." (Matthew 5:21–44).

Every head turned to follow his finger as Jesus drew their attention to a few carefree birds flying overhead. They were featherweights in the lineup of things that matter. He pointed out that they "do not sow or reap or store away in barns, and yet your heavenly Father feeds them" (Matthew 6:26). Maybe those little creatures were invisible to most people, who were busy with their lives and in a hurry, never noticing them, and yet Jesus told the crowd that God sees them. They matter to God.

If God cares for these fragile bits of fluff that might seem so insignificant in the big scheme of things, how much more does he care for you! Here's how Jesus said it: "Look at the birds of the air: they neither sow nor reap nor gather into barns, and yet your heavenly Father feeds them. Are you not of more value than they?" (Matthew 6:26 ESV) and "Are not two sparrows sold for a penny? Yet not one of them will fall to the ground outside your Father's care" (Matthew 10:29).

If God cares for these fragile bits of fluff that might seem so insignificant in the big scheme of things, how much more does he care for you!

After almost twenty years of being confined to a bed, Civilla's friend could have felt invisible, sidelined, and bitter for the life that didn't happen. But that wasn't her focus. She may not have been able to see *why* she suffered, but from her bed she could look at the birds and see the absolute truth that she mattered to God. Her trust in God didn't require understanding her circumstance.

Her heavenly Father wasn't like the dad whose eyes are on the screen of his phone as his son tries to get his attention. "I'm listening," the distracted dad assures the boy. Finally, in frustration the boy tells his dad, "Listen to me with your eyes, Daddy."

She knew her heavenly Father was listening to her with his eyes. His eyes were focused on *her*. She knew she had his full attention. It would have been easy for her to believe God had abandoned her or that God was against her or punishing her.

Instead, she was basking in her Father's attention, buoyed above the dark waters of depression by a continuous conversation with the One who made her life and her words consequential.

Not only that, but she didn't allow others to determine her worth based on false scales for assessing value: How smart are you? How capable are you? How beautiful are you? How gifted are you? How wealthy are you? How famous are you? How many likes do you get on social media? What can you do for me? Instead, she chose to rest in the assurance that her heavenly Father loved her and was watching over her. She realized her worth in a relationship with the One who made her and saw her as his treasure.

I wonder whether there are days when you feel like the sparrows Jesus talked about. The eyes of people who seem to matter look past you as if you're not there. You speak, but your words go unheeded. I wonder whether years of not being heard and feeling overlooked has led you to believe something about yourself or about God that isn't true. Maybe things have happened to you that make you feel broken and worth less than what you once knew to be true. Sometimes we're tempted to think our value is determined by the rank we hold, the perks we enjoy, the number on the paycheck we deposit, or the person we're with. Myths like these suck the joy out of life and create an arid place where the very things we need to live evaporate. If you're struggling to survive in a desert like this, come to this oasis and drink deeply.

It doesn't matter what your circumstance, your disability, your pain, or your past may say about your worth.

It doesn't matter how far you've missed the mark of what or where you wanted to be on this earth.

It doesn't matter what scars you carry, weary warrior.

Here's the truth—your heavenly Father sees you, and you are his treasure.

Before you let someone else decide your significance, consider what you're worth to God. What must your value be in light of these truths?

> God showed how much he loved us by sending his one and only Son into the world so that we might have eternal life through him. This is real love—not that we loved God, but that he loved us and sent his Son as a sacrifice to take away our sins. (1 John 4:9–10 NLT)
>
> What marvelous love the Father has extended to us! Just look at it—we're called children of God! That's who we really are." (1 John 3:1 MSG)

You can be sure God is for you because . . .

Your heavenly Father sees you, and you are his treasure.

PRAYER

Father, I am not defined by my disabilities or my failures. While I may feel that I am invisible to others, I know you see me. The truth is, you designed me, and I am your treasure. Knowing you love me unconditionally, I choose to live a life overflowing with hope and joy. Lord, would you let a bit of the hope and joy you've given me spill over onto someone you bring across my path today? In Jesus's name. Amen.

TALK IT OVER

1. Describe a time when something or someone made you feel unseen or unloved.

2. What helps you know God sees you and values you? That you are God's treasure?

3. What is the source of your self-worth?

4. What would you say or do to help someone who feels invisible or worthless?

SONGS TO LIFT YOUR SPIRIT

"The God Who Sees," featuring Nicole C. Mullen

"How Deep the Father's Love—Songs from Home"
by Phil Wickham

Chapter 6

OUTLIERS AND OUTCASTS

If we walk in the light, as he is in the light, we have fellowship with one another, and the blood of Jesus, his Son, purifies us from all sin. If we claim to be without sin, we deceive ourselves and the truth is not in us. If we confess our sins, he is faithful and just and will forgive us our sins and purify us from all unrighteousness.

1 John 1:7–9

Levi was definitely an outlier. Somehow, steeped in the same Jewish culture as the others, he turned out, well, different. He wasn't much when it came to fishing or farming, but Levi did have a knack for taking complex matters and putting them all in order. He was also a stickler for keeping accurate accounts of things. When he saw the chance to leverage his gifts for big bucks, he took it. It was a golden opportunity for a guy like Levi, but there was a catch. He knew it would cost him his friends, his family, and the respect of his community. No matter. There was too much money at stake in this deal. If it meant being the *second* most despised man in town, so be it.

So who was the most hated man in Capernaum? That would have to be Herod Antipas. Levi signed on to work for Antipas, the ambitious, wily fox (Luke 13:32) who ruled Galilee for Rome for more than forty years. When a young woman caught Antipas's eye, he divorced his wife and married her. There were several details that made this relationship complicated. His first wife was the daughter of King Aretas, who wasn't pleased with the humiliation of his daughter and declared war on Antipas as soon as she was safely home. Antipas's new wife? That was complicated too. Her name was Herodias, and she was none other than his niece and had been the wife of his half brother Philip. (It's generally believed that Philip and Herodias divorced.) When this shady relationship turned up in some of John the Baptist's fiery sermons, Herod Antipas had John arrested and then beheaded, at the request of Herodias's daughter—whom Herodias had told to ask for John's head (Matthew 14:1–12).

Levi's job was collecting the taxes that would flow into Antipas's coffers to fund his lavish lifestyle and grand building projects. There were taxes on fish and any commodities produced in Galilee.[1] But most days Levi manned the booth where he collected the tolls and customs fees. These were required for anything that moved on the Roman-built road running past Capernaum, a prosperous fishing town of about fifteen hundred people that was well situated on the Sea of Galilee's north shore.

The network of roads connecting Rome with the empire was one of the great engineering marvels of its day. The wide stone-paved highways were an awe-inspiring upgrade from the trails they replaced, and their ruins remain to this day. One road in particular was a vital artery for commerce, creating one of the most important trade routes in the world. It started in Damascus, Syria, ran through Capernaum in Galilee, then went along the Mediterranean coast, all the way down to Egypt. A superhighway in its day, today it's known as the Via Maris, or Way of the Sea.[2] With plenty of trade and traffic moving through Capernaum, it was the perfect spot for Levi to cash in.

Roman soldiers were there to enforce Roman law and maintain control. They were available to back up Levi in the collection of taxes and customs. It was no secret. Everybody knew that Levi and his fellow tax collectors were gouging citizens and getting rich off the backs of their own people. To most of Capernaum, Levi and his ilk were nothing more than thieves. Even worse, they were traitors, collaborating with pagan occupiers to satisfy their own greed. Righteous anger rose up inside the good people of Galilee when they saw someone like Levi the tax collector.

Levi's story took a dramatic turn when Jesus made Capernaum his home base in Galilee. Jesus recruited several disciples in and around Capernaum. Brothers Peter and Andrew, along with brothers James and John, were there, making their livings with fishing businesses. You have to agree that if you're putting together a team to change the world, these four fishermen are certainly interesting choices. But it turns out they were just the kind of guys Jesus put at the top of his list.

If you were to include all the people of Capernaum on that list in order of their suitability for the band of twelve brothers Jesus would call to follow him, who do you think would be *last* on the list? Start at the top and run your finger all the way down until you reach the last name. There he is. Levi. No doubt he'd be the least likely candidate in Capernaum to get an invitation to be a friend of Jesus and join his disciples. Hated by the religious folks of Capernaum, surely Levi was someone God would be pleased to see cast out and suffering the scorn of his community. Certainly Levi's coldhearted greed had earned him a spot on God's hit list.

The scene could hardly have been more dramatic. Jesus stopped at the toll collector's booth and looked at Levi, the son of Alphaeus. Just the guy he was looking for. Maybe it happened as it's depicted in Caravaggio's famous painting *The Calling of Matthew*. The artist's brush brought the moment to life. Jesus entered the shadowy room with a shaft of light and pointed to Levi and said, "Follow me" (Luke 5:27).

The incredulous tax collector, one of the chief villains in town, could hardly believe his ears. He had one hand on his money and with the other pointed to his chest, as if to say, "Who, me? You must have the wrong guy."

I'm sure Peter and Andrew, James and John, and the others were just as stunned as Levi. To everyone's amazement, in a miraculous moment of awakening, Levi stood, walked away from his cash cow and the source of his security, and followed Jesus (v. 28).

I suspect, somewhere along the way, Jesus must have given Levi a new name. Jesus seemed to have a penchant for assigning nicknames. Simon became Cephas, "the rock." That one fit him so well it has stuck through the centuries in its Greek form, Peter, "the rock." To James and John, he gave the colorful name Boanerges (pronounced bo-ner-gees), the Sons of Thunder. Another good one. Wouldn't it be fun to know how they earned that nickname? Maybe it was the time they suggested calling down fire from heaven to destroy a Samaritan village that would not accommodate Jesus because he was a Jew on his way to Jerusalem (9:54). Sons of Thunder seemed to fit. Hmm, now Levi. What to call him? I love that Levi, entering the group with a reputation that stunk to high heaven, became Mattityahu, or Matthew, "gift from God."

SIMON'S STORY

Jesus picked up another outlier for his team when he called a second Simon to follow him. This one was not the rock. This Simon was the Zealot. This Simon was on fire. He was passionate about his hatred of Romans and anyone friendly with the Romans. He may have been part of a group that worked covertly to disrupt Rome's occupation of their homeland. They were called the Zealots. They wanted Rome's pagan influence out of Israel.[3]

They wanted to be free from Roman control, and they were willing to use violence to achieve their purpose. They were certain they were on the side of righteousness and confident of God's endorsement.

Are you following this? Jesus just chose a thieving collaborator who was collecting taxes for Rome and a fiery Zealot whose mission in life was to do whatever it took to kick the Romans and their Jewish collaborators out. One was passionate about Jewish tradition and keeping the law. The other was passionate about making money. I'm thinking I wouldn't put these two in the same town, much less in the same small group. Yet Jesus invited both. He loved both. He knew both needed a Savior. In Levi's greedy thievery and Simon's hard self-righteousness and boiling political passions, they had both missed the mark of what God required—by a mile. They both had the Ten Commandments. They also had the message God had sent them through the prophet Micah.

> He has shown you, O mortal, what is good.
> And what does the LORD require of you?
> To act justly and to love mercy
> and to walk humbly with your God.
> (Micah 6:8)

Against these standards, they were both guilty. Yet there was an invitation and an offer of forgiveness waiting for both.

Jesus included two guys on his team who were living on different planets. One was fire, the other gasoline. Surely he knew there would be an explosion. Didn't he spend all night in prayer before he selected his apostles, the ones he would soon send out two by two to heal the sick and call people to turn from their sin and believe in him (Luke 6:12–16)? And he chose these two? Yes, he did. But he didn't just call them to follow him. He also called them to be brothers who loved each other and followed him together. And they did. Spending time with Jesus and each other, these two started to change from the inside out.[4]

It inspires me how Jesus transformed ordinary guys in the middle, like Peter and his brother Andrew and so many others. But I have to tell you that I find great hope in how he transformed the ones on the fringes, guys like Levi the tax collector and Simon the Zealot. He didn't just change their hearts and behaviors. He transformed their relationships with one another. Do you realize they weren't devoted to Jesus only? In time, they were devoted to one another. Little by little, the things that energized them before they met Jesus faded. More and more, their deepening trust in Jesus and loyalty to him crowded out every other passion and priority (Acts 1:12–14; 2:1).[5]

Jesus didn't just change their hearts and behaviors. He transformed their relationships with one another.

It still works like that when we follow Jesus. This song always moves me: "Turn your eyes upon Jesus. Look full in his wonderful face, and the things of earth will grow strangely dim in the light of his glory and grace."[6]

When Jesus calls us to follow him, there's always the beautiful promise of wiping the slate clean of our messy pasts. We're all ready to sign up for that. There's also the promise of victory over death and the bright hope of a place reserved in heaven. Yes please! Sign me up for that too. But we can't stop there, because there's more. The call to follow Jesus and be reconciled with God is also a call to be reconciled with one another. You can't accept one and leave the other. When Jesus called Levi to follow him, it wasn't just a "me and Jesus" thing. It was a "me and Jesus and a whole community of Jesus followers" thing. He called him to be part of a family, a community, a band of sisters and brothers all caring for one another.

If you're someone who has walked with Jesus for a long time, have you discovered Jesus doesn't use just the contacts on your phone as suitable candidates to make out his invitation list to follow him? Sometimes he invites someone on the other side of the political fence, someone with crazy ideas, or someone with a scandalous lifestyle, and he says to them, "Come, follow me." He invites people into the family who don't think like you. He welcomes people onto his team who don't look like you. Sometimes it's like they show up from another planet to follow Jesus *with you*. What do you do with that?

SIDE-EYES AND SIDEBARS

I wonder whether Jesus ever caught Simon giving Matthew a look. You know the kind. One of those side-eyes. Have you ever caught someone looking askance at you? Or maybe you were the one looking with disapproval because of someone's clothes or hair or accent or tattoos or crude language. I wonder whether Jesus ever overheard Simon passing along a morsel of juicy gossip about Matthew's days as a tax collector. I'm sure there were some stories to share. It's not hard to imagine Jesus having a little sit-down with these two former enemies to remind them of what they had just heard him teaching the crowds:

> Do not judge, or you too will be judged. For in the same way you judge others, you will be judged, and with the measure you use, it will be measured to you.
>
> Why do you look at the speck of sawdust in your brother's eye and pay no attention to the plank in your own eye? How can you say to your brother, "Let me take the speck out of your eye," when all the time there is a plank in your own eye? You hypocrite, first take the plank out of your own eye, and then you will see clearly to remove the speck from your brother's eye. (Matthew 7:1–5)

Maybe in one of those sidebar sessions, Jesus went deeper to help Matthew the tax collector and Simon the Zealot see the bigger picture of what he came to do.

The apostle Paul caught a glimpse of Jesus's mission of reconciliation and wrote about it. He was speaking of how God brings Jews and Gentiles together in Christ. His words could also apply to any community, church, or nation that finds itself divided into hostile camps. It could even be the members of your family who have taken sides and dug in, determined to defend their truth.

> For Christ himself has brought peace to us. He united Jews and Gentiles into one people when, in his own body on the cross, he broke down the wall of hostility that separated us. He did this by ending the system of law with its commandments and regulations. He made peace between Jews and Gentiles by creating in himself one new people from the two groups. Together as one body, Christ reconciled both groups to God by means of his death on the cross, and our hostility toward each other was put to death. (Ephesians 2:14–16 NLT)

HOOAH!

I deployed to Prince Sultan Air Base (PSAB), Saudi Arabia, as the senior chaplain in the summer of 1999. From its humble beginning in the early nineties as Al Kharj (or Al's Garage, as airmen in the early days liked to call it) to the time I arrived, PSAB had grown into one of the Air Force's largest expeditionary operations in the world, with more than five thousand airmen assigned. It was a sprawling base located about fifty miles into the Arabian desert from Riyadh, where it was conveniently out of sight for most Saudis. The expansive concrete apron next to the flight line was filled with scores of aircraft from several countries parked wingtip to wingtip. Hardworking ground crews were launching these aircraft around the clock to enforce the UN-mandated no-fly zone over Iraq. PSAB was the busy hub for air operations in Operation Southern Watch.

I settled in, met my team of eight chaplains and five chaplain assistants, and paid a visit to the commander. Our mission at PSAB was to care for the thousands of Americans rotating in and out at four- to six-month intervals or longer. With the exception of the commander and a few others who were often on the job seven days a week, most everyone else worked six twelve-hour shifts every week with one day to rest, work out, and run errands. I would fall into the same rhythm with my team.

My first day on the job, a sergeant showed up at my office wanting to talk to a chaplain. Bill grew up rough, passed from house to house, and was mostly raised by his grandparents. Church had never been even the smallest part of his life. He was a firefighter—or a fire dog, as he and his buddies called themselves. He had arrived at PSAB several months before with a big load of baggage. It wasn't the kind you can see, but real nonetheless. He was in a dark place when he'd deployed, producing pornography and dabbling in the occult. He confessed that his marriage was in shambles. Just several nights before I arrived, he finished his shift at the firehouse and caught a ride back to his quarters several miles away. Walking through Coalition Complex that Friday evening, he saw a group of people enter a building he hadn't noticed before. There was a rock standing nearly as tall as a man at the entrance with the words *Desert Hope Chapel* on it. Curiosity and boredom drew him in. As he opened the door, he heard loud and lively music. *This could be good,* he thought.

He followed the group inside and started up a flight of stairs right behind them. At the top, he took a right turn and followed them into a large open room filled with people. The others took a seat, but he decided to stand in the back until he knew more about what was going on.

Bill had walked in on the Gospel Explosion chapel service. It was one of more than a dozen different services we offered each week to accommodate the schedules and religious backgrounds of as many airmen as possible. Every Friday night this service attracted a large and faithful congregation and a talented team of volunteer musicians. Feeling more comfortable and enjoying what seemed simply like a free concert, Bill found an open seat in the back and sat down. After the singing, a young man about his age, who was a regular at that service, spoke about things Bill had never heard before. As his fellow sergeant talked about the grace of God, Bill heard for the first time how Jesus died on the cross to pay the penalty for all *his* sins. He could be forgiven of every shameful, hurtful thing he had said and done. He could get a fresh, clean start. When an invitation was given to come forward for prayer, Bill stepped out and knelt at the front along with several others.

"It felt so awkward. I didn't know anything about prayer. So, I just knelt there with my eyes closed," he later said to me.

> **Bill heard for the first time how Jesus died on the cross to pay the penalty for all *his* sins. He could be forgiven of every shameful, hurtful thing he had said and done.**

An officer named Markus was also there that night. Unlike anything Markus had experienced before, he felt a nudge from God to go kneel beside Bill and pray for him. So he did. As his knees touched the floor, he felt another nudge to put an arm around Bill. So he did. He felt compelled to pray for this stranger he'd not seen in the service before. As he prayed, Markus was overwhelmed with emotion.

Bill listened to the fervent whispers of the man at his side as he talked to God about him. Then he opened his eyes and looked down at the mottled, beige tiled floor beneath him. "Chaplain, when I opened my eyes, I saw something that changed everything," Bill told me.

I couldn't imagine what he had seen in the tile and wasn't sure what to expect. "What did you see, Bill?"

"I saw tears," he said. "I saw tears falling on the floor as this stranger prayed for me. In my whole life, no one had ever cried for me, Chaplain. I can't explain it, but when I saw that, it was like all my defenses came tumbling down. I wanted to be forgiven for all the stuff I'd done. I knew I needed to start over, but I didn't believe that was even possible before Friday night. I never imagined that God would accept someone like me."

As I listened to Bill, I realized God had done something totally unexpected. If you had made a list of all five thousand people at PSAB that summer and put them in order of who was most likely to show up in chapel and announce a decision to follow Jesus, Bill may have been last on that list. But he was at the top of Jesus's list. How often Jesus walks past those who would seem like obvious choices, then stops and points at a guy like Levi or Simon or Bill or me, and says, "Come, follow me!"

Why do you think that is? Don't ever believe that you—or someone you love—is beyond the grace of God. I believe there's an invitation to follow Jesus with your name on it.

While they were both on the same military team, when Markus and Bill walked into the chapel that Friday night, you might say they were divided by rank, religion, and race. One was an officer, and the other a sergeant. One was a deeply committed Christian, and the other was toying with Satanism. One was Black, and one was White. Only God knows their hearts and how they saw each other. What matters is this: When they walked out of the room that night, they were brothers in Christ.

You know what I think? If Jesus called Matthew the tax collector and Simon the Zealot to follow him as brothers *together*, if they were able to serve him and others together, if they gave their lives away together, and if they loved each other because Jesus first loved them despite all their faults and failures, then there's hope for your family, your community, and our nation.

After he told me his story, Bill got to the reason for his visit. Markus had spent some time with him and talked with him about the next steps after his decision to follow Jesus. He asked me if I would baptize him.

> **Don't ever believe that you—or someone you love—is beyond the grace of God.**

"Bill, it would be my great honor to baptize you," I told him.

We set a date for his baptism in the swimming pool right across the street from the chapel. A chaplain assistant made the arrangements with the team that managed the pool, and we were all set.

When the big day arrived, Bill showed up early. He didn't come alone. It seems he told everybody who would listen about his decision to follow Christ and invited them all to his baptism. He told his supervisor and his fire dog buddies. He told the guys at the fitness center tent. He told his roommates and the guys up and down the hall. The dramatic change in Bill must have piqued their curiosity, because a big crowd showed up to witness Bill's baptism. The lifeguard in charge blew a whistle and shouted for everyone to get out of the pool. Everyone climbed out of the water without complaint and watched from the side, along with Bill's friends, as five men in shorts and T-shirts took the steps into the shallow end of the pool.

Bill was first. I introduced him to the curious onlookers, many wrapped in towels. "Bill, are you trusting Jesus as your Savior?" I asked loud enough for all to hear.

"Yes, I am," he answered confidently.

"What is your confession of faith?" I asked.

Bill was ready with his response: "Jesus is Lord!"

"Bill, on your profession of faith in Christ and in obedience to his command, I baptize you, my brother, in the name of the Father, the Son, and the Holy Spirit." Then as I lowered Bill into the water, I proclaimed the truth we could already see happening in Bill's life. "Buried with Christ in baptism. Raised to walk a brand-new life."

I could have stopped right there. But I didn't. Giving everyone a chance to affirm Bill's decision to follow Jesus, I called out to the crowd gathered around the pool, "And all the people said . . ."

Now, I was anticipating they would finish my statement with a hearty amen. But that's not what I got. Bill's friends shouted in unison, "Hooah!"

It was a great day at PSAB.

You can be sure God is for you because . . .

Jesus invites you to follow him.

PRAYER

Lord, sometimes I think of my own brokenness and wonder how you could love me or invite someone like me to follow you. Other times, in arrogant self-righteousness, I wonder how you love someone who doesn't think just like me. Yet I know, Lord, we all need your grace. I acknowledge I have sinned against you. Help me receive your grace with humble gratitude and offer it freely to others who have hurt or offended me. When I think about how you know my every word and deed and even my thoughts, I'm amazed you invited me to follow you and to love everyone you love. I ask this in Jesus's name. Amen.

TALK IT OVER

1. What person, book, song, or circumstance is God using—or has he used—to invite you to follow Jesus?

2. How is God's invitation to follow Jesus evidence that God is for you?

3. Is there a broken relationship God wants you to mend? What is a first step you could take toward reconciliation?

4. How would you help someone who is considering following Jesus but is put off by the Christians they know?

A SONG TO LIFT YOUR SPIRIT

"One Day" by Cochren & Co.

Chapter 7

HOPE LIKE WATER

Let us hold unswervingly to the hope we profess, for he who promised is faithful. And let us consider how we may spur one another on toward love and good deeds, not giving up meeting together, as some are in the habit of doing, but encouraging one another—and all the more as you see the Day approaching.

Hebrews 10:23–25

Though one may be overpowered,
two can defend themselves.
A cord of three strands is not quickly broken.

Ecclesiastes 4:12

We were a band of brothers, David, Wayne, and I. Along with our boom operator, we made up a combat aircrew flying KC-135s, known as tankers. We were stationed at Travis Air Force Base, near San Francisco. During those days in the Strategic Air Command (SAC), we might fly together for several years as a hard crew instead of being mixed and matched with others.

Not only were we assigned to fly every mission together, we were also scheduled to pull alert together. Every third week we holed up for seven days behind concertina wire in a squat, above- and belowground alert facility next to the flight line. We would arrive with bags loaded with gear and take our seats in a briefing room for a weather report and classified intelligence briefing. Our crew was matched up with one of the five gray behemoth tankers lined up in a row facing the runway, each one loaded to the max with about 180,000 pounds of jet fuel.

From the alert facility, we walked the short distance to our plane, climbed the ladder into the cockpit, and went through a preflight checklist. The other four crews did the same. Soon the tankers sat cocked and ready to launch within minutes in case of a missile attack on the United States.

A portion of the first morning was always spent locked in a secure room. With the crew gathered around a table, I'd open a brown leather attaché case marked *Top Secret*, and we'd study a mission we hoped we'd never fly. Our primary job in those days was deterrence. Paired with a bomber and its aircrew also on alert somewhere in the US, we were ready to make an attack so costly, no enemy would be willing to try it. This was Cold War combat.

There was a reason for assigning us as hard crews and not as individual pilots, navigators, and boom operators with a different mix for each mission: safety. The idea was that if we always worked together as one team, we'd form a stronger, safer crew. Our mission success and safety record proved it worked.

I'm telling you all this because there was another outcome to the hard crew concept. We bonded. Our families also became close. On alert weekends, when we were allowed to have visitors, our wives would come out and spend a couple of hours with us. We sat around in a plain but spacious family room and watched our kids crawl around on the well-worn carpet, building up their little immune systems. During those evenings on alert, Wayne, Dave, and I would play some serious cutthroat racquetball and endless games of spades. We probably wouldn't have admitted it at the time, but gradually we grew to love each other.

When we weren't on alert, we were together flying five- and six-hour training missions over California, Oregon, Nevada, and Arizona. We'd fly to the appointed refueling track, rendezvous with our receiver—often a B-52 bomber—and off-load up to fifty thousand pounds of fuel. From there we'd fly a ninety-minute route I had planned out the day before to practice celestial navigation. Once those duties were complete, we'd head back to home base, where the pilots practiced takeoffs and landings, squeezing in as many touch-and-gos as possible before our landing time. For some new copilots, touch-and-gos could be more crash-and-dash. There were a few times I felt sure we'd cheated death.

Sometimes we'd be tagged for a TDY (temporary duty) and head west across the Pacific, dragging fighters at thirty thousand feet. Over water, the F-4s would stay close on our wings. When their fuel ran low, they'd drop back to refuel on our boom, then return to their positions in the formation on our wings. That was how we made our way from Travis to Hickam Air Force Base, Hawaii, to Andersen Air Base, Guam, and finally to Kadena Air Base, Japan. In those days, with no GPS or computer onboard, navigators really earned their money on those transpacific flights. Armed with a compass, a chart (map), a watch, an airspeed indicator, my mechanical pencil, and a sextant to take shots on the sun, moon, and stars, I was working nonstop from takeoff to landing.

That was more than forty years ago. Although we've kept in touch through the years, this summer, for the first time, the three of us and our wives gathered at our house for a reunion.

Before they all arrived, I set out a photo of our crew from back in the day. It was taken while we were on alert, to be used in a briefing Dave and I were supposed to do Huntley-Brinkley style for some visiting civilian dignitaries. (Go ahead and google Huntley-Brinkley, if necessary.) We were in our flight suits out on the wing of an alert bird, our backs to the fuselage. The boom operator and copilot were standing, while the pilot and I were both on one knee in front of them. The blue Strategic Air Command patch was proudly emblazoned on the plane to our right. It was a money shot.

Before our friends arrived, my grandkids studied the picture. Then they looked questioningly at me and back at the photo again. They're still not convinced I'm really in that picture. To tell you the truth, I don't recognize myself either. Age has done its work on all three of us, but I can tell you this: The camaraderie we felt as young crew dogs is undiminished. It was as if no time had passed. We stayed up late telling war stories, most of which were true. And we remembered friends who served with us. That's what old warriors do.

Old warriors repurposed! Wayne (pilot), Bob (navigator), and Dave (copilot) forty years later, ready to grill burgers for our Fourth of July reunion.

AN OLD SOLDIER REMEMBERS

Near the end of his life, King David's thoughts went back to the mighty warriors who had served with him when he was a young commander. The faces of valiant heroes and stories of high-risk missions came rushing back to him in a flood of nostalgia. Decades after they had faced death together in combat, David's love and respect for these brave men was undiminished. I can understand that. There's something about military service, particularly combat experience, that forms an enduring bond between warriors. The writer of 2 Samuel recorded one of David's stories. He wanted us to know that these were "the last words of David" (23:1).

> During harvest time, three of the thirty chief warriors came down to David at the cave of Adullam, while a band of Philistines was encamped in the

> Valley of Rephaim. At that time David was in the stronghold, and the Philistine garrison was at Bethlehem. David longed for water and said, "Oh, that someone would get me a drink of water from the well near the gate of Bethlehem!" So the three mighty warriors broke through the Philistine lines, drew water from the well near the gate of Bethlehem and carried it back to David. But he refused to drink it; instead, he poured it out before the LORD. "Far be it from me, LORD, to do this!" he said. "Is it not the blood of men who went at the risk of their lives?" And David would not drink it.
>
> Such were the exploits of the three mighty warriors." (vv. 13–17)

This story has long fascinated me. Let me give you a little of the background. Several centuries after Moses led the Hebrews out of Egypt and into the land God had promised them, David was still fighting Israel's archenemy, the Philistines. Apparently, it was not going well. David was hiding in a cave while the Philistines were living their best lives with their headquarters in Bethlehem, which happened to be David's hometown.

People and places dear to David were under the control of a brutal enemy. Despite his apparent disadvantage in the conflict, he had determined that he would liberate Bethlehem. I suspect at this point David must have been running a bit low on hope for carrying out that mission. It could be that he saw his men were discouraged and on edge about the collision with the Philistines sure to happen soon. Maybe both were true. Imagine with me the questions no one spoke: *Are we fighting a losing battle? Are we headed for defeat and death?*

Great military leaders—and David would certainly fall into that category—depend on clear, precise communication with their troops. But in this case, David dropped a cryptic message within earshot of some of his men. "Oh, that someone would get me a drink of water" (v. 15). There's nothing that would be unusual about his being thirsty and asking for water, but notice that not just any water would do. He specifically wanted water "from the well near the gate of Bethlehem" (v. 15). This wasn't really a thirst for water at all. David wasn't dehydrated. On that day his greatest need wasn't water. What he needed was an infusion of hope.

THIRSTING FOR HOPE

I wonder whether someone near you or maybe someone dear to you is in a battle. You can see they're discouraged. You know they're wondering how much longer they can hold out for a breakthrough. Maybe they haven't told you, "I'm discouraged" in so many words. Maybe you've never heard them admit, "I'm afraid." But you can decipher the cryptic messages. Maybe you are the one with the unspoken cry for help. Are you that someone needing an infusion of hope today? I think that's where David was.

> **David's greatest need wasn't water. What he needed was an infusion of hope.**

Why do you think David wanted water from that particular well in Bethlehem? It wasn't because it tasted better than water from any other well. It wasn't about some sentimental notion of water from home. Just imagine what a flask of water taken from a town in the grip of the Philistines might mean to David and his band of warriors. And not just any water from Bethlehem. This would be water from the well "near the gate" (v. 15).

I don't think you have to have a military background to figure this one out. Let me ask you a question: Where is security tightest on a perimeter? If you said, "At the gate," you'd be correct.

In military parlance, that's the ECP, or the entry control point. Then and now, armed guards defend the gate, always on the lookout for anything suspicious.

It could mean certain death for one of David's men to show up at that particular well. But what if, against all odds, someone could penetrate Philistine defenses and bring back water from the well by the gate? That water would deliver a message loud and clear. It would certainly be a miracle and a game changer for David and his men. It would shout to them, "Don't be discouraged. Don't lose heart. God is with us. With God all things are possible!" It would satisfy a thirst for hope no other water could quench.

The word of David's thirst reached three of his chief warriors. Knowing the risk, three heroes stepped forward together and said, "Let's roll!"

PRICELESS WATER

I happen to be writing this chapter on September 10. Tomorrow will mark the twentieth anniversary of the 9/11 attack on the United States. Some have called that attack the Pearl Harbor of our generation. I remember that day so well. I remember where I was and how I felt. I also remember 9/12. It was a time when our country was as united as I've ever witnessed in my lifetime. Perfect strangers helped each other. Lawmakers from both parties stood *together* on the steps of the Capitol and sang "God Bless America." Go ahead and take a moment to savor that image. Churches were filled. Mighty men and women from across America heard their nation's call and stepped up to defend her.

It was my privilege to serve as a chaplain to thousands of those who joined the military in direct response to the terrorist attack that left almost three thousand innocents dead and shattered the lives of their families. I've deployed to Saudi Arabia and Iraq with them. I've traveled to Kyrgyzstan, Qatar, and Afghanistan to encourage them. I've seen their courage and selfless heroism firsthand. Coming from every corner of this nation, they were all so different. What they shared in common was a noble sense of duty to defend our country. They were mighty men and women indeed. It was my great honor to serve with them. I loved being their chaplain.

I believe they were cut from the same cloth as David's selfless, fearless, loyal warriors. No wonder he called them "mighty" (2 Samuel 23:16). Knowing it might cost them their lives, David's men set out on a mission impossible. But an amazing thing happened. It's something that happens every now and then when, against all odds, a team stands up and says, "We'll go—whatever the cost!"

Well, a miracle happened. Somehow they broke through the lines and drew water from the well by the gate at Bethlehem. They carried it back to David, their leader. I've often wondered how they did it. Did they use deception? Maybe they employed a distraction. I suppose we'll never know how they did it. What we do know is that they did it *together*, as a band of brothers. Isn't it amazing what good can be done when a team of people can rein in their egos, grow to trust one another, and work together for something larger than themselves? Notice we don't even know the names of these three warriors. Sometimes miracles happen when people serve together without concern for who gets the credit.

Imagine with me the celebration when the three intrepid warriors entered the camp with the water held high above their heads. Did David do one of his famous dances? Did their brothers surround them and lift them onto their shoulders, shouting victory? Whatever their responses, it was a moment David treasured for the rest of his life. In fact, it's what was on his mind during his final days on this earth.

Now, here's how I know this was never really about David's physical thirst: When they presented the water to David, did you see what he did with it? He wouldn't drink it. Instead, he poured it out. Why on earth would he do such a thing? Great question.

Here's why: He refused to drink it for the same reason we have Memorial Day to remember and honor those who died to keep us safe and free. David poured the water out for the same reason a monument stands in Shanksville, Pennsylvania, to the memory of those heroes on Flight 93 who gave their lives on 9/11 so that others would live.

Who can forget the final words of a hero named Todd Beamer, a thirty-two-year-old software salesman who spoke to Airfone operator Lisa Jefferson for fourteen minutes after he and other passengers figured out their flight was being hijacked? They realized the plane they were on was likely going to be used as a weapon of destruction against the Capitol. They were told three other flights had already been flown into the World Trade Center towers and the Pentagon.

Mene Ukueberuwa, writing for *The Wall Street Journal*, recounted the phone conversation that happened between Todd and Ms. Jefferson that fateful day. As I read it again, it transported me back twenty years, and I felt the same surge of emotion as I did then.

> Before ending his call with Ms. Jefferson, Beamer asked, "Would you do one last thing for me?"
>
> "Yes, what is it?" she answered.
>
> "Would you pray with me?"
>
> They said the Lord's Prayer together in full, and other passengers joined in. Beamer then recited Psalm 23, concluding, "Yea, though I walk through the valley of the shadow of death I will fear no evil, for thou art with me." Immediately after, he turned to his band of brothers and asked, "Are you guys ready? Okay, let's roll."[1]

Today, in the field where they brought the plane down, stands a beautiful memorial to the heroes of Flight 93 who gave their lives that September day. It was necessary for us to dedicate that sacred ground to their memory and acknowledge their sacrifice. How could we do otherwise? How could we not respond to such a gift that cost others their lives?

When the water from Bethlehem arrived in the camp, David asked himself a similar question: "'Is it not the blood of men who went at the risk of their lives?' And David would not drink it" (2 Samuel 23:17). He couldn't take that flask of water, gulp it down, and wipe his mouth with his sleeve, as if risking their lives meant nothing to him. This water was priceless. Three souls were willing to die to put this water in his hands.

What happened next is significant. David poured the water out—not casually as if he really didn't want it. I believe what he did was not waste but a solemn act of worship. Can you picture it? He must have called his band of brothers together, and they had church. The climactic moment was when David lifted the flask of water to the Lord and emptied it (v. 16). It was entirely appropriate for David to worship God in response to what the daring warriors had done. Here's why: David knew they could never have done this without God's help. He saw God's fingerprints on a miracle like this. David knew he had asked for something that was beyond their reach. He had asked for something humanly impossible, and God chose to take the opportunity to show up and do something only God could do.

When his three triumphant troops entered the camp with the water from Bethlehem, David saw the undeniable evidence of God's favor right there before him in plain sight. In fact, here was hope they all could see. Even from the dark cave where he was hiding for his life and dreaming of the liberation of people dear to him, he and his troops could see something now they couldn't see before. They could say with confidence, "The Lord is with us. The Lord is for us. With God's help we will prevail!"

WHAT'S YOUR STORY?

Many of you could tell a story of being in a desperate situation. You were sick, helpless, broken, running out of options, and growing weary in the battle. You were hunkered down in fear and running low on hope. Then someone came to you with an encouraging word, a timely gift, or a comforting presence. It may have been a small thing to them, but to you it meant the world. Even if what they did didn't change the situation you were in, it changed the situation in you. It restored your hope.

Never discount the value of a kind gesture or an uplifting, life-giving word to someone who is facing hard circumstances and running low on hope. It may seem like a small thing to you—just a cup of water in Jesus's name—but to the one suffering in a dark place, it just may turn on the light of hope.

> **Never discount the value of a kind gesture or an uplifting, life-giving word to someone who is facing hard circumstances and running low on hope.**

I want you to remember this: Where was David when he was pouring out the water before the Lord in worship? He was still in the cave, and the Philistines were still in Bethlehem. His situation was unchanged. But now he had hope, and that made all the difference, and it moved him to worship. Don't miss that.

You're still facing a financial crisis. The diagnosis of a chronic illness remains the same. The other side of the bed is still empty. Someone you love is still held captive by an addiction or still fighting some other battle. But here's what's different: When God restores your hope, you can see a truth you couldn't see before. Now you know you're not in this alone. The myth that you're in this battle by yourself has been busted. You can say with confidence, "I know God sees the crisis I'm in today. I know he cares. I know God can and will help me."

Maybe for the first time, or the first time in a long time, you want to bow your head and tell God what's in your heart. Would you make the words of this prayer your own?

Even though your circumstances may not have changed, you can be sure God is for you when . . .

God restores your hope.

PRAYER

Lord, right now I don't know how you're going to win this battle I'm in, but I'm trusting you. I'm grateful for my family, for my church, and for the friends who care about me. Through their kindness and sacrifices, Lord, I can see that you are with me. And because you are with me, I won't give up, and I won't let fear rule over me even when I'm walking through a valley of dark shadows. I'm ready to take the next step with your help. Thank you for opening my eyes to see the truth that you are with me in this battle. Thank you for restoring my hope. In Jesus's name. Amen.

TALK IT OVER

1. Share a time when your family, church, or group of friends was there to support you when you were going through something hard. Whatever they did for you, how did it help you go on even if it didn't change your circumstances?

2. Who has sacrificed something to help you? Describe the circumstances and how their help changed you.

3. How have you expressed gratitude for the sacrifices others have made for you?

4. Is there someone you know who would be encouraged with a small gift, a meal, a card, or some other

expression of kindness, even if it may not change their circumstance? What steps can you take in the next day or two to reach out to them?

SONGS TO LIFT YOUR SPIRIT

"Stay Strong" by Danny Gokey

"There's Nothing That Our God Can't Do" by Passion, Kristian Stanfill

Chapter 8

JESUS, JOB, AND BUBBA

For I am about to do something new.
See, I have already begun! Do you not see it?
I will make a pathway through the wilderness.
I will create rivers in the dry wasteland.

Isaiah 43:19 NLT

Our oldest granddaughter is happiest when she's far from the lights of the city with her canine companion, Georgia. On a weekend you might find them hiking a high-country trail or paddleboarding on the clear waters of a mountain lake. Yesterday, she texted a video to the nine people in the family group chat we call "Fam Bam." In my unbiased opinion, this clip could land her and Georgia a reality TV show called *Backroads Washington*. She, with her faithful wonder dog at her feet, was in a wilderness somewhere, standing in a postcard-worthy mountain stream. She had set up her phone to perfectly frame herself in the video, displaying an expert fly-fishing technique. Then in a made-for-TV moment, she pulled in a beautiful little steelhead trout. The only sounds were the rushing of the water and her excited squeals of delight. Nearby sat her trusty nine-year-old Ford Escape with the back hatch open, providing an excellent view of the camper conversion she and her pops had rigged up for her wilderness adventures.

When we use the word *wilderness* today, we imagine an unspoiled, beautiful place like this, somewhere far from the stress of our workaday life, a place of peace and serenity. It's the kind of place you see on someone's social media in a vacation selfie—a picturesque lake reflecting the vibrant colors of wooded mountains and blue skies.

This wasn't at all the image of wilderness in biblical times. In the Old and New Testaments, wilderness was a place of hardship, struggle, and loneliness. It was no one's happy place. It was often the crucible where a person was tested physically and spiritually.

Eventually we all spend time in a wilderness. I'm speaking of the biblical kind. The setting of your wilderness may vary. It may be your apartment in the city, your home in the suburbs, or your place at the end of a country lane. It can be the office where you work or a hospital room. But sooner or later trouble finds you and you're there.

Let's look at the wilderness experiences of three well-known characters in the Bible: Jesus, Job, and Bubba. Oh yes, Bubba's there. Read on, and I'll introduce you to him shortly. The first question we ask when we find ourselves in a wilderness experience of the biblical variety is why. *Why am I going through this? Why has God allowed this pain in my life?* Let's look into these wilderness experiences for some answers.

TEACHER OF THE YEAR

Jesus spent forty days and nights in the wilderness where he was tested. Matthew tells us when Jesus was hungry, he was tempted to use his power to turn stones into bread. He crushed the temptation by remembering truth God had already given him: "Man shall not live on bread alone, but on every word that comes from the mouth of God" (Matthew 4:4). Then he was tempted to reveal himself as the Messiah in a spectacle by throwing himself off a high place. Having memorized this clear guidance from Scripture, Jesus was ready to quash that idea. "It is also written: 'Do not put the Lord your God to the test'" (v. 7). Finally the devil offered him an earthly kingdom—with a catch. The kingdom would be his in exchange for his worship.

Isn't there always a catch? Behind the instant gratification and the shiny object dangling in front of you is an addiction or the loss of things you once treasured. But Jesus didn't take the bait. He dispatched the tempter with this direction from God's Word: "It is written: 'Worship the Lord your God, and serve him only'" (v. 10).

Before those hard days in the wilderness, Jesus had spent time in God's Word. He had memorized these verses in Deuteronomy, so he was ready to do spiritual combat with the Enemy we all face. Psalm 119:11 was his strategy for dealing with temptation: "I have hidden your word in my heart that I might not sin against you."

There's a remarkable verse in the book of Hebrews. I'm sure I don't yet understand its full meaning, but I believe it offers us insight into why God allowed Jesus to spend forty days in the wilderness and suffer through other hard times common to all of us. The writer of Hebrews told us, "Even though Jesus was God's Son, he learned obedience from the things he suffered" (5:8 NLT). That's an incredible statement. Jesus experienced what we all go through. He learned what it's like to be human and deal with appetites, impulses, and ego just like we must. He experienced life as we know it, in full measure and with its heartaches and hard times. For example, the death of his earthly father, Joseph, isn't mentioned in the Gospels, but it seems sometime before Jesus began his ministry at about age thirty, Joseph must have died. Jesus would have suffered grief and the pain of loss. Many believe he was the eldest son in a household with his widowed mother for some years. He knew hard times. Then he deployed to the wilderness. Far from family and friends. Hungry. Tempted to take the shortcut. Doing battle with a treacherous enemy. Through it all, what he learned made him the perfect One to stand between us and the Almighty.

I would say to my brothers and sisters in arms, Jesus has been to the desert. To all I say, Jesus knows the wilderness where you find yourself. He understands what you're going through. He gets us. The writer of Hebrews said it like this: "This High Priest of ours [Jesus] understands our weaknesses, for he faced all of the same testings we do, yet he did not sin" (4:15 NLT).

> **Jesus knows the wilderness where you find yourself. He understands what you're going through.**

Just as hardship, suffering, and loss prepared Jesus for his role of representing God to us and us to God, your hard times can prepare you for the good work God has for you. Several years after I retired, a friend still on active duty called me out of the blue. He was going through a difficult time. I listened to his story. It was one that sounded familiar to me. I shared some encouraging words and prayed with him. Before he said goodbye, he thanked me. "Bob, what you said was on target, just what I needed to hear."

Any idea why I understood his situation and how I was able to tell him the things he needed to hear? You guessed it. I had gone through something similar in my career.

Look at this: "Blessed be the God and Father of our Lord Jesus Christ, the Father of mercies and God of all comfort, who comforts us in all our affliction, *so that* we may be able to comfort those who are in any affliction, with the comfort with which we ourselves are comforted by God" (2 Corinthians 1:3–4 ESV).

These words open the letter the apostle Paul wrote to his friends in the city of Corinth. These were friends he had introduced to faith in Jesus. Now they were going through hard times. Paul had gone through similar *affliction*, as he called it. He could understand what they were going through and wrote one of the most encouraging letters in the New Testament to them. He began by tracing the path of comfort. It all flows from God, who is the ultimate source of, or the Father of, compassion. That's where mercy and comfort begin—with God. Now follow its journey from there. It flows from God to you *so that* you can share it with others.

Here's the truth I want you to see: When you've been through the school of hard times and suffering, there could be a mission with your name on it. God can repurpose the trial you're going through and equip you for a good work that will help others. Ask any one of the scores of families with a child, teen, or adult with disabilities who flock to our church on Sundays. They'll tell you Wendi Akers is a hero. For years she has been the driving force behind a ministry called iFit, which has created an amazing place for kids on the autism spectrum and others with special needs. A big team of volunteers helps her every week. They'll all tell you that Wendi is the one with the answers, the know-how, and the understanding to make it all work. Families with a kid on the spectrum tell me she is an answer to their prayers. Want to know how she developed this superpower? You guessed it, of course. She and her husband raised a daughter with autism.

There's another important lesson for us when we go through something hard. Paul told us what he learned going through a situation so dire he thought he would not survive it. "We do not want you to be uninformed, brothers and sisters, about the troubles we experienced in the province of Asia. We were under great pressure, far beyond our ability to endure, so that we despaired of life itself. Indeed, we felt we had received the sentence of death. But *this happened that we might not rely on ourselves but on God*, who raises the dead" (2 Corinthians 1:8–9).

No one has demonstrated greater mastery of this lesson than Jesus. Again and again he revealed his utter dependence on the Father to direct and empower his every word and deed. "The Son can do nothing of his own accord," he said, "but only what he sees the Father doing" (John 5:19 ESV). And how did he see what God was doing? He prayed. Before he chose his disciples—kind of a big decision—he prayed all night (Luke 6:12). Once he told a crowd questioning him about his identity, "When you have lifted up the Son of Man, then you will know that I am he and that I do nothing on my own but speak just what the Father has taught me" (John 8:28). He was relying on God to do what seemed impossible. When others would lift up to die on a cross, God would lift him up from the grave and draw many to experience a new life through his death and resurrection (John 12:32).

> **God can repurpose the trial you're going through and equip you for a good work that will help others.**

Enrolled in the same school of suffering, Paul learned not to rely on himself but to depend fully on God. That's the only thing that made sense in that situation. When circumstances are beyond your control and death is staring you in the face, what can you do? Let me speak for Paul. "In those times of extreme hardship," I think he would tell us, "I learned to trust God like I had never trusted him before. Because I was certain God had raised Jesus from the dead, I knew I could trust him through the terrible thing I was going through—even if it cost me my life."

Paul was confident and capable, gifted with extraordinary intellect, energy, and courage. His natural impulse would certainly have been to rely on his own abilities. It took going through a flood of high-pressure hardships that overtopped his abilities for him to grasp how to switch his power source from his own strength to God's far greater strength.

Through his own suffering, Jesus blazed a clear trail to hope for you and me. Paul walked that same road to hope and described it for us in his letter to the believers in Rome. "We also glory in our sufferings, because we know that suffering produces perseverance; perseverance, character; and character, hope" (Romans 5:3–4). As we rely on God through our hard times, he develops spiritual stamina in us. Then, as we remain steadfast in faith through our suffering, God develops in us the character of Christ. Now look what happens at this point on the road. We begin to experience the confident assurance that what God has said, he can and will do. This hope is the firm expectation, regardless of the circumstances, of a better day, knowing God is always faithful to his promises. Because God is for us, we can be sure our pain will not be wasted.

THE GUEST NO ONE INVITED

Job was a rich man with a big family. Then his life started to sound like a country music song. In one tragedy after another, he lost his wealth, his health, and his family. His wife tried to help, and said, "Why don't you just curse God and die!" (Job 2:9 ERV). I'm sure she meant well.

Friends came to help. They accused him of doing something really bad. The loss of his reputation as a man of integrity must have been like salt in his wounds. But that's often the idea, isn't it? When something bad happens, it must be punishment for something you've done wrong. That's such a hurtful thing to say to anyone, including yourself. I hope you'll let me bust the myth that God's main job in the universe is punishing wrongdoers and that's the reason you're suffering now. In Job's case, we know his suffering wasn't because of anything he had done wrong. God loved Job and never left him. God's purpose in allowing Job's suffering was known only to God.

That's often the way it is. There are times we suffer, and there's no understanding why. I can't tell you why a family is taken in a highway accident. Or why a good man gets a diagnosis of pancreatic cancer. Or why a young woman suffers with brain tumors. Or why a baby has to have an arm amputated to save his life. But I've seen all these things happen and more. Maybe we'll understand someday. I pray we do. But for today it's part of living in a broken world. The truth is, cancer happens to people who are kind and generous, people who love their families and put the needs of others before their own. Tragic accidents, cancers, or a hundred other terrible diseases can happen to them, like they do to anyone else.

I got a call some time ago. The voice on the other end of the line lamented the fact that he had been trying to do right, and bad things were still happening to him. His car and his wife's had both broken down in the same week, requiring expensive repairs they couldn't afford. To add insult to injury, some family members were saying hurtful things about him that weren't true. He felt like giving up on faith in God. "Others are out there doing terrible things," he said. "I'm here trying to do good. Why does this stuff happen to me? Is God mad at me or something?"

Jesus gave us advance notice that following him doesn't exempt us from hard times. Just the opposite. He said, "In this world you will have trouble" (John 16:33). Truer words were never spoken. In fact, Jesus said people may insult you, persecute you, and say mean things about you simply because of your connection to him (Matthew 5:11). I don't know why cars break down when we can least afford it. What I do know is God doesn't abandon us in our suffering, and he will bring us through our wilderness if we trust him.

> **I don't know why cars break down when we can least afford it. What I do know is God doesn't abandon us in our suffering.**

When I heard of this man's trouble, I thought about how hard times provide opportunities for us to help one another. (Just not the way Job's wife and friends did.) For example, one day Jesus and his disciples encountered a man who had been born blind.

When Jesus looked at this man, he saw an opportunity to do the good works God had sent him to do, and he healed him. When his disciples looked at the man, they saw a theological question. "Who sinned, this man or his parents, that he was born blind?" (John 9:2). They were thinking, *Surely this man or his parents did something that angered God, and his terrible condition is the consequence.* They were so confident in their understanding of how the world worked that they didn't ask *if* the man or his parents sinned but *who* sinned to cause his blindness. They were thinking, as we sometimes do when we are suffering, *This must be happening because God is punishing us.* Jesus set them straight. The man's blindness had nothing to do with his sin or his parents' sin (v. 3). They were asking the wrong question. They should have been asking, "How can we help?"

Job didn't give in when he lost his wealth. He didn't give up when he lost his health. He didn't let go of his faith in God even when he lost his family. He never waved the white flag of surrender, except to the One. Now that's remarkable when you consider that unlike you and me, Job knew nothing about the life, death, and resurrection of Jesus. That wouldn't happen until centuries later. Even though he had a limited knowledge of God, what he did know was enough for Job to choose to trust God in his suffering. Job said, "I will continue to trust God even if he kills me" (Job 13:15 ERV). It was in trusting God through his wilderness of tragedy and suffering that Job found hope. That's why after thousands of years we're still talking about this hero of faith and resilience. After all he suffered, after all he lost, look how Job's words still brim with hope.

> I know that my redeemer lives,
> and that in the end he will stand on the earth.
> And after my skin has been destroyed,
> yet in my flesh I will see God;
> I myself will see him
> with my own eyes—I, and not another.
> How my heart yearns within me!
> (19:25–27)

CHOICES HAVE CONSEQUENCES

Luke 15:11–31 introduces us to a character I'll call Bubba. As the baby of the family, Bubba had a pretty good life. His father put up some fences to keep him safe. "Son, don't go out there," he said. "You can have fun on this side of the fence."

But Bubba kept looking over those rails. It looked like all the good stuff was on the other side. Bubba grew up and became a man with big appetites. He was hungry for pleasure. Hungry for possessions. Hungry for power over his own life. He wanted to be free to do what he wanted when he wanted and not answer to anyone. Bubba thought, *I know I'd be happier on the other side of this fence.*

He pondered that day after day. Then one day Bubba came up with a plan. He went to his father and told him, "Daddy, you know that stuff I will inherit when you die? Why don't I just take it now?"

When his father gave him what he asked for, he packed up his stuff and left home. His travels took him a very long distance from his father's house. At first it was all he dreamed it would be. He was free to do what he wanted when he wanted and answer to no one. He was free to satisfy his appetites for pleasure and possessions. The burden of responsibility, the boredom of routines, and those frustrating fences were all far away back home. It was so good—until it wasn't.

One day his friends were all gone. His money was all gone too. It seemed to Bubba they left about the same time. Times were hard, and Bubba was hungry. He got a little job feeding pigs. It wasn't the position he dreamed of, but it was just temporary until he could get back on his feet. Day after day he fed those pigs. He resented that they ate better than he did. Days turned to weeks and weeks into months. More and more, Bubba felt shame for the things he had done and who he had become.

Something he heard back home came to mind. "*Sin always takes you farther than you want to go, costs you more than you want to pay, and keeps you longer than you want to stay.*" He remembered how he had scoffed at that saying. But now he understood what it meant. He thought of how far he was from the place where he grew up.

Meanwhile, back at the farm, Bubba's father would walk out the front door every day, and the screen door would slam behind him. He'd walk to the edge of the porch and stand with one hand shielding his eyes as he searched the horizon, yearning for his boy to come home. Days turned into weeks and weeks into months. The old man's steps got slower and his hair turned white, but he still stood on the porch each afternoon, hoping this would be the day Bubba came home. He knew in his heart he would gladly sacrifice his own life if that would bring his son home.

Ask any mom or dad with a wayward son or daughter for the thing they yearn for most, and they'll tell you it's what happened next. One day, there with the pigs, Bubba came to his senses. He saw things in a whole new light. He came up with a plan. He said, "I'll go talk to my father. I'll tell him, 'I'm not worthy to be your son anymore. Would you just let me work for you like one of your hired hands?'"

That day, like all the others, the father stood at the edge of the porch, peering into the distance where the road bent, watching for his boy. Then someone came into view. Could this be Bubba coming home today, after he had watched for him for so long? The man looked like his son. He walked like his son. *It's him! It's Bubba! He's come home.*

His father didn't wait for Bubba to reach the house. Here's how Jesus told it. It's the best part of the story: "But while he was still a long way off, his father saw him and was filled with compassion for him; he ran to his son, threw his arms around him and kissed him" (Luke 15:20).

Jesus wants you to know *that's* what God is really like. Regardless of what you've heard, where you've been, or what you've done, this is the Father he wants you to know. You may have had a wonderful dad who loved you unconditionally, who was generous in his affirmation of you, and who was always there for you—but I know many didn't. Your dad may have been physically or emotionally absent or abusive. For you it may be difficult to even imagine a God who expresses his love for you, who is kind and generous and always there for you. Yet this is exactly the God Jesus showed us in his story of the son who left home and the father who joyfully welcomed him back. He gave us a stunning, myth-busting, truth-revealing, life-changing picture of a *running* God. He upended all our errant ideas about God and let us see the Father's heart. When a wayward son showed up smelling like pigs, what did his father do? He didn't hesitate. He ran to him and embraced him right there, just like he was—dirt and stink and all. There was no judgment or condemnation. There was only grace. I don't know what ideas you have about who God is and how he responds to broken people. Can you imagine God running to embrace somebody as messed up as this kid was? Jesus could.

Bubba's father didn't see the wealth that was lost or the years that were wasted. He only saw the son who had been lost was now found. He put a clean robe on his boy. He put a ring on his finger, and he threw a party for him (vv. 22–23). *My son has come home! He was dead and now he's alive!*

Even after growing up in his father's house, it's easy to see that Bubba never really knew his father at all. If he had really known his father's heart, he would have left that pigpen and run home long ago.

You can be sure God is for you because . . .

God doesn't waste your pain but uses it to accomplish good.

PRAYER

Father, I know we live in a broken world where Jesus said there is trouble. Please use these difficulties to teach me to depend on you and help me grow in ways I'd never be able to otherwise. Lord, repurpose my pain to equip me to help someone else. When my choices have taken me far from you and I'm suffering the consequences, help me to turn my back on my old, self-directed ways and return to you. Thank you for the promise that if I confess my sins, you are faithful and just to forgive and cleanse me, and welcome me home. In Jesus's name I pray. Amen.

TALK IT OVER

1. Jesus, Job, and Bubba each spent time in a different wilderness. When has life been like a wilderness for you? Where is the wilderness for you now?

2. What lessons did you learn (or are you learning) in your wilderness?

3. Why is it such a struggle when bad, unfair, or senseless things happen to us or to people we care about?

4. How would you help someone dealing with the consequences of bad choices?

5. How would you help someone who is struggling to understand why God has allowed something difficult or painful in their life?

A SONG TO LIFT YOUR SPIRIT

"Run to the Father" by Matt Maher

Chapter 9

YOUR NEW BEST FRIEND

I will ask the Father, and he will give you another advocate to help you and be with you forever—the Spirit of truth.

John 14:16–17

I have called you friends.

John 15:15

One of our favorite couples from our Air Force days is Jon and Peggoty (pronounced Peg-a-tah) Stovall. Peggoty has what I would call a muscular faith. There's hardly any other way to describe how she trusts God through the challenges she has faced in life.

As a young woman, Peggoty had an experience with God and responded with a deep, enduring commitment to live out the words from the prophet Isaiah:

> The Spirit of the Sovereign LORD is on me,
>   because the LORD has anointed me
>   to proclaim good news to the poor.
> He has sent me to bind up the brokenhearted,
>   to proclaim freedom for the captives
>   and release from darkness for the prisoners,
> to proclaim the year of the LORD's favor.
> (Isaiah 61:1–2)

Peggoty knew how Jesus stood in the synagogue in his hometown of Nazareth and read those very words from the Isaiah scroll one Sabbath morning. Then to the amazement of the congregation, Jesus applied those ancient words to himself. With everyone's eyes riveted on him, he sat down and announced, "Today this scripture is fulfilled in your hearing" (Luke 4:21; see also vv. 16–20).

On a day that changed everything for young Peggoty, the Holy Spirit spoke through those same words to call her to follow Jesus and spend her life caring for people and sharing the good news of God's love. Peggoty was quick to respond in much the same way young Isaiah, the author of those words, did when God called him to serve: "Here am I. Send me!" (Isaiah 6:8).

Not long after the birth of their first child, Peggoty started having vision problems, which got significantly worse with the birth of their second child twenty-two months later. After multiple appointments and tests, finally there was an answer. But it was not the answer she wanted to hear. A diagnosis of multiple sclerosis left her confused and angry at God. She lamented, "God, I'm doing the best I can to serve you and do what you called me to do! Haven't I been faithful to share your good news with others? Haven't I worked hard to help others see the truth of your Word and find freedom in Christ, just as you called me to do? How do you expect me to do these things and care for my family while MS is robbing me of my vision and strength?"

She didn't hold back as she battled with God. Apparently, God wasn't put off by her strong words. Instead, after pouring out her heart to God and venting her anger, she felt the overpowering presence of the Holy Spirit comforting her and filling her with peace. In the quiet that followed, the Holy Spirit spoke gently to her heart, "If you don't know what it's like to be blind, how will you care for those who are?"

Having come to terms with the diagnosis, Peggoty determined this: "I will live the best life for the Lord and my family that I can for as long as I can."

Her struggle continued without relief for almost twenty years, until one day she was gripped with the searing pain of a debilitating headache. It was unlike any other headache she'd ever had. From her experience as a nurse, she knew something was wrong in her brain. Scans soon revealed that her vision problems, and now this excruciating headache, were not caused by MS. She and Jon were hardly prepared for the shocking news. The scan revealed four tumors growing in Peggoty's brain. Two of them had grown large. But it was a smaller one wrapped on the optic nerve of her right eye that was causing the greatest problem.

At the time, Jon was assigned as a chaplain to F. E. Warren Air Force Base in Wyoming. A surgeon nearby removed the two large tumors. When a surgeon in San Antonio, Texas, said he could remove the two smaller tumors, including the one on the optic nerve, and spare her eye, Jon and Peggoty traveled to San Antonio to have him do the next surgery. Although Peggoty realized she would lose her vision in her right eye, she was grateful she would be able to keep that eye. What Jon and Peggoty didn't know was that yet another shock was waiting for them. In a surgery that took more than sixteen hours, the surgeon removed the tumors, and in the process he found two aneurysms in her brain. He was able to clip one. The other would have to be carefully monitored and removed in yet another surgery.

Jon's next assignment took him to Germany, and Peggoty was

medically cleared to join him there. Once they were settled in, a German doctor made the next discovery that upended their lives. He told them Peggoty had an arteriovenous malformation in her brain, and at that moment she was at great risk the AVM would rupture. The doctor told her there were only a handful of surgeons in the world who could help her. She would need to return to the States to deal with this latest setback.

Stunned, Peggoty left the doctor's office and went home feeling like her strength was gone. She had been in this battle for more than twenty years, and now her energy had simply drained from her. She walked in the door, collapsed onto the couch, and let her head fall back. She knew she needed to talk with her heavenly Father and lay this all out before him, and before that day she would have. But she didn't have the energy to pray. "Lord, I'm so tired. I'm bone weary" was all she could get out.

There was no anger. There were no questions. There was just utter exhaustion. She was physically and spiritually spent. Feeling weaker and more vulnerable than ever before, she closed her eyes. Then once again, in the quiet, a familiar voice spoke to her heart. The Holy Spirit's soothing words may have been inaudible to her, but they were undeniable. The One Jesus had promised to be with her and live within her said, "Rest, my child." Then he spoke words she has cherished ever since, "Rest in the prayers of my people. My people all over the world will be praying for you. You just rest, my child."

Jon and Peggoty flew from Germany to Washington, DC, where they met a doctor at Bethesda Naval Hospital (Walter Reed National Military Medical Center). He explained the innovative procedure he planned to use. As Jon held his wife's hand, they listened intently. Instead of surgery, he would thread a catheter all the way to the site of the malformation in her brain and use a surgical glue to seal off the tangle of veins and prevent them from rupturing.

The day before the surgery, Peggoty got a call from Hawaii. She immediately recognized the voice of her dear friend Vickie, also an Air Force chaplain's wife. She knew firsthand that Vickie was a woman of great faith and a dedicated prayer warrior. Vickie had called to let her friend know she would be praying throughout the entire four-hour procedure that would take place the next day. Shortly after Peggoty talked with Vickie, Jon's phone buzzed with a message from a dynamic young chaplain they knew back in Germany. He had mobilized the community there to pray for Peggoty. Not long after that, a fellow chaplain and his wife from the Chief of Chaplains office in the Pentagon stopped in to visit. They came with a simple message to encourage Peggoty and Jon. "We want you to know the team at the chief's office will be praying for you, dear friend," the chaplain said.

> **The One Jesus had promised to be with her and live within her said, "Rest, my child. . . . Rest in the prayers of my people."**

In that moment Peggoty knew what the Lord had spoken to her back in Germany had just been confirmed. His people—people all over the world—were praying for her. From Hawaii, prayers were rising to the Father for her; in Washington, DC, they were asking God to bless her and her husband; in Germany, they were fervently calling her name to God; and in so many other places around the world, God's people were coming together to pray for her. She knew the Holy Spirit had been faithful to his promise. Comforted by that and his presence, she would do as he had directed her—she would rest in the prayers of his people and not fret or fear.

When I asked our dear friend if I could share her story, Peggoty didn't hesitate. "Of course," she said. "It's not my story, but God's story."

She responded to my question about her continuing battle with recurring tumors, and added, "If you want to see what answered prayer looks like, look at me."

There's that muscular faith I told you about.

THE PROMISE OF ANOTHER FRIEND

In the final days of his ministry on earth, Jesus met with his friends to prepare them for the shocking events about to happen and the hard times he knew were just ahead. "Do not let your hearts be troubled," he told these dear ones he loved "to the end" (John 14:1; 13:1).[1] Along with the troubling news that he was leaving them, he made them a promise: "If you love me, keep my commands. And I will ask the Father, and he will give you another advocate to help you and be with you forever—the Spirit of truth. The world cannot accept him, because it neither sees him nor knows him. But you know him, for he lives with you and will be in you" (14:15–17). Then Jesus did something beautiful. He blessed them with his peace, and he guaranteed the One he was sending them would teach them the things they would need to know and remind them of the things Jesus had told them. It was a dark night, and as they huddled around the light that was soon to leave them, Jesus repeated the words he knew they needed to hear: "Do not let your hearts be troubled and do not be afraid" (v. 27).

Continuing to reassure his disciples, Jesus called them friends (15:15). As evidence of their friendship, he pointed out how he had disclosed to them everything he had learned from the Father, including the promise that with his departure, God would send another advocate to be with them. For three years he had been their advocate, but now he was leaving. However, he would not leave them as orphans to face the hard times on their own. He wouldn't let them flounder, trying to love and obey him on their own. He would send another advocate to help them do the daunting task he had given them and face the trials about to come upon them. The Holy Spirit would love them, help them, guide them, teach them, and correct them just as Jesus had done. The meaning of this word *another* is that the Holy Spirit would be an advocate of the same kind. He would be a friend just as Jesus had been. More than a doctrine to be endorsed in their heads, the Holy Spirit was to be their new best friend, dear to their hearts. And he's just the kind of friend you want to have with you when you're in trouble or facing hard times.

Do you remember how Jesus gave special names to his disciples, revealing something about their characters or missions? There was Simon who became Peter, "the rock." There was Levi, who became Matthew, "gift from God." Who can forget Boanerges, Sons of Thunder, for James and John? Jesus also used a special name to introduce us to the Holy Spirit. He called him Paraclete, which can be translated "Advocate," "Helper," or "Comforter."[2] In using that name for the Holy Spirit, Jesus wants you to know that the One he promised God would send you is no ordinary friend. He is someone called to come alongside you as your faithful advocate, someone who will passionately plead your case for you, and someone who will advise and help you when you're facing circumstances that call for more wisdom or strength than you have.

When Jesus used the name Paraclete, he wasn't telling you the Comforter will pat you on the back and tell you everything is going to be all right. Yes, the Holy Spirit consoles us in our grief, but he does so much more. Take the syllables apart and look at *fort*. When we say the Holy Spirit is the Com-*fort*-er, we mean he *fortifies* us or strengthens us from within. Jesus wants you to know the Comforter will supply courage when you are discouraged and power when you are weak. In fact, the Holy Spirit brings the same awesome power that raised Jesus from the dead to your need. Yet you need not fear One so powerful moving in to take up residence in you. Jesus wanted his disciples to know this friend would not be someone different from the Lord they had known and loved. He would be another just like Jesus, "full of grace and truth" (John 1:14). He is, in fact, the Spirit of Christ.

While his friends were grieving his departure, Jesus made a statement that must have shocked them. He told them, "It is for your good that I am going away" (16:7). What? How can that be? There was something he wanted them to experience that was even better for them than his physical presence. How is it possible that anything could be better than being able to sit with Jesus, like Mary did (Luke 10:38–39 and John 12:1–3)? What could be better than being able to see and hear him, like John did (1 John 1:3)? Imagine the privilege of being able to say, "We have seen his glory, the glory of the one and only Son, who came from the Father, full of grace and truth" (John 1:14). What could be better than that? But Jesus told them, "It is for your good that I am going away. Unless I go away, the Advocate will not come to you; but if I go, I will send him to you" (16:7).

How could their experiences with the Holy Spirit be better for them than walking and talking with Jesus? And what does that matter to us? Great questions! Here are four beautiful benefits in his gift of the Holy Spirit that were available to those first disciples of Jesus and remain available for you and me today.

First, the Holy Spirit would be not only *with* them but *in* them. He would live within each one of them and be on duty 24/7 to help them with every challenge they faced. You have to admit, this was taking their relationships with Jesus to a new level. He would not just be with them here and there or now and then, as Jesus had been. The Holy Spirit would be with them everywhere all the time. Limited by a human body just like you and me, Jesus could only be in one place at a time. But the Holy Spirit can be, and is, with each and every one of God's people all at once. Jesus could exert his influence by placing himself where someone could see him, hear him, or touch him. But the Holy Spirit, wherever he is welcome, will take up residence in believers and guide each one from within. More than some external earbud whispering truth to guide you through the day, the Holy Spirit is an indwelling source of power and encouragement always available to help you be who God has called you to be and do the things God has planned for you to do.

Second, the Holy Spirit helps us see the truth about ourselves and Jesus. Since Jesus made the bold claim, "I am the way and the truth and the life" (John 14:6), it should not surprise us when he introduces the Holy Spirit as the Spirit of truth: "When he, the Spirit of truth, comes, he will guide you into all the truth"

(16:13). As we read God's Word or hear it being read, the Holy Spirit will open its truth to the seeking heart.

If we allow him, the Holy Spirit will help us see things about ourselves we've not seen before. He will convince us of our need for a Savior. Jesus said, "[The Holy Spirit] will convict the world concerning *sin* and *righteousness* and *judgment*" (v. 8 ESV). Notice Jesus said the Holy Spirit's focus here isn't on the wrong things we've done (sins, plural). Instead, the Holy Spirit goes beneath the behaviors to the condition of our hearts, to our sin (singular) problem. The Holy Spirit's work that Jesus is speaking of here is not shining a light on bad behavior but exposing our sin of disbelief. The Holy Spirit helps us see that we've broken the heart of the Father by rejecting the love he has shown us in his Son.

> **The Holy Spirit is an indwelling source of power and encouragement always available to help you.**

This would be terrible news if the Holy Spirit left us there, with an awareness of our sin and our separation from God without a remedy. The good news is that he doesn't leave us to despair. He will always point us to Jesus and reveal a right relationship with God that is *received,* not *achieved.* Now that's not just good news—that's wonderful news! In Christ, the Holy Spirit shows us a righteousness that is never achieved through good works but always received through faith. Paul said it this way, "This righteousness is *given* through faith in Jesus Christ to all who believe" (Romans 3:22). The Holy Spirit helps us see that right standing with God is a gift to be received instead of a reward to be earned. Jesus forever freed us from earning. "All have sinned," Paul told us, "but the *gift* of God is eternal life in Christ Jesus" (v. 23; 6:23).

Jesus said the Holy Spirit would also convince us of *judgment.* Don't misunderstand and think he was threatening impending doom here. No, this is not a judgment to come.[3] This is a judgment that has already happened in Christ's death on the cross. He has paid the debt we could never repay, and he has defeated the Enemy of our souls. "The ruler of this world is judged" (John 16:11 ESV). The Enemy's doom is certain. The war has already been won through the death and resurrection of Jesus.

The Holy Spirit doesn't just help us see ourselves as we are—his greatest work is helping us to know the truth about Jesus. Jesus said of the Holy Spirit, "He will glorify me" (v. 14). In our darkness, the Holy Spirit will always shine a light on Jesus so we can see he is God with us. He is God for us. And in the Holy Spirit, he is God within us, the hope of glory.

Third, the Holy Spirit confirms you are God's dearly loved child. When we respond to the gentle nudges of the Holy Spirit and let him lead us, look at the wonderful thing he does for us: "Those who are led by the Spirit of God are the children of God. The Spirit you received does not make you slaves, so that you live in fear again; rather, the Spirit you received brought about your adoption to sonship. And by him we cry, '*Abba*, Father.' The Spirit himself testifies with our spirit that we are God's children" (Romans 8:14–16).

The fourth way the Holy Spirit helps us is one of the most practical and beautiful benefits of all. In our human weakness, there are times when we are facing sickness or loss or loneliness or a question we can't answer, and we don't know which way to turn. There are times we have no idea what to ask for or how to pray. But the Holy Spirit understands us completely. He sees our every flaw and weakness. He also knows the will of God for us. In our distress, he stirs within us so that even in our weakness, even in our agony, our groaning rises to God as a prayer God will understand and answer. Paul told us, "The Spirit helps us in our weakness. We do not know what we ought to pray for, but the Spirit himself intercedes for us through wordless groans. And he who searches our hearts knows the mind of the Spirit, because the Spirit intercedes for God's people in accordance with the will of God" (vv. 26–27).

FREE FOR THE ASKING

Peggoty's story and her walk with Jesus inspire all of us who know her. But her experience with the Holy Spirit—the way he speaks to her through God's Word, the way he encourages her and gives her the strength and courage to take the next step, the way he confirms that she is God's dearly loved daughter, and even the way he directs others to pray for her—is not unique to our friend. In fact, every part of that has been the experience of God's people ever since the Holy Spirit made his debut at Pentecost. I can also say that has been my experience in following Jesus, and the good news is that experience is available to everyone who asks.

IS THIS A GOOD TIME?

Imagine going to a friend's house at midnight to borrow bread. You knock on the door and try to explain your problem to your friend by shouting through the door. Earlier that evening, like other young parents, your friend went through a seven-step bedtime routine with his three kids. They're all asleep now, and he lets you know he's not happy you're pounding on his door and shouting loud enough to wake the whole household. However, not one to give up easily, you keep knocking and calling his name with "shameless audacity" (Luke 11:8). Finally, knowing there will be no sleep until you get what you came for, he gets up and gives you the bread (vv. 5–8).

Jesus told that story (or something like it) because he wants us to know God is nothing like your sleepy friend. Whenever and wherever we call on him, God loves to hear our prayers, and he delights in giving us what we need. He invites you and me to call out for his help with shameless audacity. After telling the story of someone's midnight call on a neighbor to ask for bread, Jesus had something to say to the fathers in the crowd. "You dads out there, as imperfect as you are, you know how to give good gifts to your children" (v. 13, author's paraphrase). The dads were nodding their heads up and down when Jesus lowered his voice. The men leaned in to hear the point of both stories: "How much more will your Father in heaven give the Holy Spirit to those who ask him!" (v. 13).

The good news is we don't have to beg God for the Holy Spirit. He is the priceless gift to every person who opens their heart to Christ. To all who put their trust in Jesus, the Holy Spirit comes to seal and secure you and stay with you. Right away he starts working in partnership with you on the project we all need to have done—transforming you to be more like Jesus from the inside out. Let me say it like this: When we receive Christ, the Holy Spirit posts a sign on your heart and mine—*This one belongs to Jesus!* Beginning that moment, he is there to guard and guide you and guarantee your safe arrival at the Father's house. What a friend indeed!

You can be sure God is for you because . . .

God gives you the Holy Spirit to guide you to the truth and help you pray.

PRAYER

Lord, thank you for calling me from my proud independence to recognize my need for you. Thank you for not leaving me alone to fight these battles on my own. Holy Spirit, your presence in my life, encouraging me and giving me strength to take the next step, is a powerful reminder that even in this difficult time, you are with me and you are for me. In Jesus's name. Amen.

TALK IT OVER

1. If you could travel in time and spend a day with Jesus during his earthly ministry, what day would you choose?

2. Jesus said the Holy Spirit would be another advocate to help you and be with you. How has the Holy Spirit helped you?

3. What is something the Holy Spirit has shown you about yourself?

4. What is something the Holy Spirit has shown you about Jesus?

5. Why do we need someone like the Holy Spirit to be with us and in us continuously?

A SONG TO LIFT YOUR SPIRIT

"Who You Say I Am" by Hillsong Worship

Chapter 10

THIS CHANGES EVERYTHING

What, then, shall we say in response to these things? If God is for us, who can be against us? He who did not spare his own Son, but gave him up for us all—how will he not also, along with him, graciously give us all things?

Romans 8:31–32

We can thank a man named John that we know Martha's story. John was with Jesus from the beginning, an eyewitness to all Jesus said and did during three years that forever changed the world. He was there to see the fascinating cast of characters Jesus met along the way. John had a gift for making these characters come alive with just a few words. Read his gospel, John, in the New Testament, and I predict Martha will walk off the page into the room where you are.

Maybe Martha was a firstborn. Like firstborns often do, she

seemed to know what her siblings should be doing. Thanks to his careful research, the erudite Luke—companion of Paul, physician, and gospel writer—turned up a classic piece of family drama involving Martha and her sister. It all played out while Jesus was visiting Martha's home in Bethany. Well, when her sister left her post helping with the meal, Martha's frustration with Mary boiled over right in front of the guests. Martha, never one to mince words, aimed her sharp complaint straight at Jesus: "*Don't you care* that my sister has left me to do the work by myself? Tell her to help me!" (Luke 10:40). Don't you love how she was ready to question what Jesus cared about and tell him exactly what he needed to do with someone whose behavior was frustrating her? Maybe you've been there.

There's another moment in the life of this family that Mark, Matthew, and then John all chose to include in their eponymous Gospels. Piecing the stories together, we know this event happened two days before Jesus's final Passover in Bethany. He was the guest of honor at a dinner in the home of a man with the unfortunate name of Simon the Leper (Matthew 26:6). Jesus was reclining at the table on a lounge, propped up on his left elbow, as they did in those days, enjoying the food Martha was serving. (Look at Martha being Martha!) While the dinner was in progress, Mary entered the room clutching an alabaster jar close to her heart. Inside the jar was a precious treasure worth more than a year's wages. She moved to Jesus's side and stood behind his head. A hush fell over the room as all the table conversation ceased. Martha paused with a tray in her hands to witness the dramatic scene unfolding before her. All eyes were on Mary as she broke open the jar. Lazarus fixed his eyes on Jesus's face, watching for a reaction as his sister carefully tilted the smooth alabaster jar over Jesus, allowing a small stream of her treasure to trickle onto his head until it saturated his hair, running down his beard and onto his robe.

John, who was often at Jesus's side at these meals, remembered how the exotic and rare aroma of the oil, infused with pure nard and likely imported from India, filled the house. Almost everyone drew in a deep breath to experience the fragrance and bask in the gracious gesture they had just witnessed. It was a beautiful tribute.

But Mary wasn't finished. She moved slowly and knelt at the other end of the couch. There must have been an audible gasp as she tilted the jar again and emptied the remainder of the costly oil onto Jesus's bare feet. Had anyone there ever seen such an extravagant display as this? But Mary still wasn't finished. She removed the cover from her head and gathered her long dark hair in her hands. Those who weren't offended by the wasteful indulgence of pouring out a year's wage onto someone's feet were surely scandalized by what happened next. Mary leaned forward until her face was almost touching Jesus's feet, and she wiped them with her hair.

She tilted the jar again and emptied the remainder of the costly oil onto Jesus's bare feet. Had anyone there ever seen such an extravagant display as this?

The warmth and beauty of the moment was marred by a blast of cold criticism released into the room. Unmoved by Mary's sacrifice, Judas condemned the waste and offered his far more practical idea of what should have been done with the valuable perfume. "Why wasn't this perfume sold and the money given to the poor?" he said (John 12:5).

John may have suspected that Judas's role as the keeper of the money bag for their group had more to do with his objection than any heartfelt concern for the poor, because Judas was a thief who couldn't resist siphoning off some of their finances for himself (v. 6).

For Mary, I suspect her scandalous extravagance and her total disregard for the demure behavior society expected of her seemed an appropriate response to what Jesus had done for her brother. (I'll tell that story a little later.) But could it be she also emptied the alabaster jar on Jesus's feet out of gratitude for what Jesus had done for *her*? Is there more to the story than meets the eye? Look with me again in the gospel of Luke.

Interestingly, Luke also shared a story similar to the one Mark, Matthew, and John told of a woman who entered the room where Jesus was a guest, reclining at the table of a host who was named Simon. Luke wanted us to know up front that Simon was a Pharisee. Just as Mary did in John's account, the unnamed woman interrupted the dinner to pour perfume from an alabaster jar on Jesus's feet. That in itself was remarkable, but she wasn't finished. She then proceeded to wipe Jesus's feet with her hair, an extraordinarily uncommon and shocking thing to do then and now. Luke didn't tell us when or where this incident happened, only that the woman was from the town where this took place. He didn't place this incident in his narrative where we would expect it to be if this woman was Martha's sister, Mary of Bethany. But then Luke may have told it out of sequence (which he sometimes does in his gospel) to draw a sharp contrast (something Luke was especially good at doing) between a proud, self-righteous Pharisee and a woman whose heart was broken over her sin, weeping and pouring out her treasure in gratitude for the grace Jesus had shown her. The unforgettable story of a woman unrestrained in expressing her gratitude for the fresh start Jesus had given her offered Luke the perfect illustration to share immediately after Jesus talked about how the Pharisees criticized him for being "a friend of tax collectors and sinners" (Luke 7:34).

Struck by the obvious similarities, scholars have long debated whether the woman in Luke's story was Mary of Bethany, the sister of Martha, as she was in John's account. While we can't say for certain that she was, we can say it is possible. And if Luke and John were telling the same story with different purposes in mind, Luke added an interesting detail that changes our understanding—and I would say our appreciation—of Mary. Luke told us the woman with the alabaster jar anointing and wiping Jesus's feet with her hair "lived a sinful life" (v. 37).

Luke also told us there were objections to what the woman did. In Luke's telling of the story, the objection came from the host, and Luke reminded us he was a Pharisee. Simon said to himself, "If this man were a prophet, he would know who is touching him and what kind of woman she is—that she is a sinner" (v. 39). In Simon's way of thinking, Jesus should have pushed her away. But Jesus didn't. We can all be grateful he is a friend of sinners.

I have chosen to imagine Mary of Bethany from the perspective of those who believe that all four gospel accounts—all of which have the woman anointing Jesus with an alabaster jar of perfume during a dinner at the home of a man named Simon—are of the same event. I include Mary's story of redemption as an encouragement for all those whose hearts are broken by the choices of someone they love. I also include her story for those who find themselves far from where they started and far from where they intended to be. With that background, I'll pick up the story on a hard day for Martha and her sister, Mary.

I think it's safe to say it was the normal thing in this family for Martha to take the lead in serving others. But on this day, it was Martha's turn to sit and let others attend to her. Tradition dictated that for seven days she should sit on a low stool to contemplate her loss and receive friends bringing food, who would be with her in her mourning. She was sitting shiva. It was not a role she accepted easily. While she appreciated the support and comfort of her community, she preferred to be doing rather than sitting and contemplating. That was especially true on the day she found herself contemplating the untimely death of her brother, Lazarus.

Her grief was complicated because, from her point of view, her brother's death was preventable. *This didn't have to happen. My brother didn't have to die like this.* Each time these thoughts pushed their way into her brain, she would be overwhelmed by a wave of grief that would swell into anger, then recede into sadness again.

Martha, Mary, and their brother Lazarus had all come to

embrace the ministry of an itinerant teacher and healer whose remarkable story aligned with the messianic prophesies they had learned as children. In fact, he had been a guest more than once in their home in the village of Bethany, less than two miles outside Jerusalem. With each visit, their friendship with the rabbi grew deeper.

It wasn't just that Jesus's parents were descendants of David, as the prophet Isaiah had predicted. Nor was it the fact he was born in Bethlehem, as the prophet Micah had foretold. It wasn't even the miracles he performed, as compelling as they were. So how was it these siblings had come to believe this man Jesus was the long-awaited Messiah God had promised to send?

Martha and Lazarus surely knew the stories of Jesus. They heard how he fed a multitude with five barley loaves and two small fish, announcing he was the Bread of Life. An eyewitness told them how he healed a man born blind and made the claim that he was the Light of the World. Certainly there was much to commend him to them, but for Martha and her brother, could the tipping point in their journeys to faith in Jesus have been something much closer to home? Could it have been the miraculous, almost inexplicable transformation of their sister, Mary? It was as if she had been captive, and now she was free.

Many times Martha and Lazarus must have agonized together about the poor choices and struggles of their sister. No matter how strongly Martha impressed upon Mary the certain disaster at the end of the path she was on, nothing moved her. Martha and Lazarus felt powerless to help their sister. It seemed to them Mary was determined to go her own way, and nothing could stop her—until Jesus!

Her siblings could not have imagined in a million years a transfixed Mary sitting on the floor at the feet of Jesus, soaking in every word as he talked about his kingdom. Even though it aggravated Martha when Mary didn't do the things she thought Mary ought to be doing, it was astonishing to see how Jesus's message of grace had pierced her heart and set in motion the most remarkable life change they had ever witnessed. Perhaps Martha's attitude was, *If you really are a changed person since you've taken an interest in Jesus, you would be in here helping me with this meal.* There's always a danger when we insist that others' walks with Jesus look like ours.

When Lazarus fell deathly ill, his sisters did all they could do to help him. As his condition grew graver by the hour, they knew their only hope was to call for their friend Jesus. They sent a young messenger to Jesus with the urgent news. Imagine how the sisters must have felt when the messenger returned without him. For some reason they could not comprehend, Jesus had chosen to remain where he was. Now it was too late. Their beloved brother was dead.

Following Jewish custom, Martha saw to it that his body was washed and anointed with fragrant nard. Within hours of his death, Lazarus was wrapped in a shroud and his face covered with a cloth. News of Lazarus's death spread from house to house in their close-knit village. Soon a crowd of wailing mourners lined the route to the family crypt.

When the young men carrying the litter with Lazarus's body arrived at the tomb, they crouched and entered the darkness. They laid the shrouded corpse on a stone shelf near the entrance, where the bodies of other family members had been laid before him. This was where the decomposing body would remain for a year. After that his bones would be interred in an ossuary, then sealed in the tomb near the other stone boxes containing the bones of his parents. The men exited the low opening of the cave and rolled a wheel-shaped stone down a sloping trench cut in the rock to seal the tomb.

With the burial complete, the seven days of shiva began. Family and friends from their village would visit daily and many others would make the short trip from Jerusalem. They came to be with Martha and remember Lazarus with stories of his generosity and piety. They came to comfort his sisters in their grief. They came to affirm their faith in a God who is sovereign.

After the burial and three days of sitting shiva, Jesus still had not arrived. As each neighbor came with food and a comforting word, Martha repeated the phrase that had become her mantra: "If Jesus had been here, my brother would not have died." At first it came out as a declaration of her faith in Jesus to her skeptical neighbors. Perhaps she even said it as a cover for her absentee Messiah. Still she fretted. Why didn't he come when she called?

Martha repeated the phrase that had become her mantra: "If Jesus had been here, my brother would not have died."

Her words are a familiar response to death. *If only* . . . If only she had done this. If only the doctor had done that. If only someone had been more attentive. It became a self-soothing placebo. *If only he had come when I called.*

The more she said those words, perhaps the less they conveyed her faith and the more they reflected her frustration. She and her family had put their faith in Jesus when their neighbors stood back in doubt. When he came to Bethany, she had welcomed him. When he and his friends showed up hungry, she had cooked for them and served them in her home. In fact, hadn't she worked without help to take care of them? Now, on the day when she needed *him,* why didn't he come when she called?

Martha bought into the popular myth that if you can control everything around you, things will be okay. The more stressful the situation became, the greater was her need to control. *Why can't people just do what I tell them to do? He should have come when I called.* Finally, on the fourth day of shiva, someone came into the house and whispered the news to her that Jesus had finally arrived and was waiting outside the village. Martha went to meet him.

Never one to mince words, Martha stood before Jesus, and the anguished words burning in her heart poured out, "If you had been here, my brother would not have died" (John 11:21). There it was. She said it. What was his answer for not responding to her call for help?

TOM'S STORY

Our friend Tom was diagnosed with pancreatic cancer several months ago at the age of sixty. For more than twenty years, Tom had volunteered faithfully at church. For the first seven years, Tom was the MVP on the road crew doing the tough, early-Sunday-morning work of setting up chairs, a stage, sound equipment, and children's program equipment. He started when the church was just beginning in a neighborhood community building. He stayed with it as it moved to a public school and finally to a much larger space at another school to accommodate the growth. It was probably the biggest mobile church set up in America at the time. Servant-hearted men and women like Tom made it work and laid the foundation for a church of eight thousand on three campuses today.

In recent years Tom had served each weekend in the children's ministry, where his wife, Dina, was the full-time staff director for preschool children. In addition, Tom became a hero to single moms at church by repairing their cars. He also earned a worldwide reputation within a global technology company for being a genius problem solver and just the man to call if you needed help. These were just a few of the many expressions of Tom's generosity.

Prayers for Tom ascended without ceasing. Prayers from his family and friends. Prayers from his pastors and a fifty-person prayer team. Prayers from complete strangers around the world. They were earnest and sincere prayers. They were prayers of faith. Most of all, day after day, Dina prayed, asking Jesus to heal her husband.

Aggressive treatment at the world-renowned MD Anderson Cancer Center in Houston, Texas, could not slow the progression of the cancer. Tom entered in-residence hospice one night so the nurses could control his pain. His family kept vigil at his bedside in shifts. Dina prayed for mercy now.

Was there no hope for Tom and Dina? Where do you find hope when the diagnosis is pancreatic cancer? Where is the hope when the doctor has exhausted every medical treatment and trial available and recommends hospice care? Could the answer be in the shocking things Jesus said and did at the tomb of Lazarus of Bethany?

BACK TO BETHANY

John, an eyewitness at Lazarus's graveside that day, gave us a vivid word picture of what happened. It almost sounds like he pulled his smartphone from his pocket and started videoing the scene unfolding before him. What was it he saw that attracted his attention?

Martha had returned to the house and told her sister Jesus wanted to see her. John zoomed in on the face of Jesus at the moment Mary arrived on the scene and repeated the words of her sister: "If you had been here, my brother would not have died" (John 11:32). I try to imagine the tone of her voice and inflection as she said these words to Jesus.

What happened next is one of the most profound moments in Jesus's ministry. He looked at Mary and saw her. He felt her hurt. He saw those who came with her and felt their grief. How did he respond? John recorded it for us with just two words: "Jesus wept" (v. 35). He wasn't sobbing or wailing like the others on the scene. John's word tells us tears were running down the face of Jesus.

When I was about nine or ten years old, I memorized John 11:35 simply because it was the shortest verse in the Bible. I thought I was so clever choosing a verse with only two words for a Bible memory game. But now, more than sixty years later, those two words are profoundly meaningful and precious to me. They tell me that God sees the one whose grief is deep and complicated, a mixture of sadness and anger. They tell me God cares about you and the loss that has left an aching emptiness in your heart.

What I understand now, which I didn't fully appreciate as a child, is that Jesus—the One who shed tears at the grave of a friend—is the Creator who put on our uniform and came to rescue us and give us hope on days just like this. John said it like this: "The Word [God] became human and made his home among us. . . . We have seen his glory" (1:14 NLT). That's who Jesus is—God dressed in human flesh.

There are so many ideas about God. But if we want to see what God is truly like, we must look at Jesus. It is Jesus who shows us who God is and what he has always been like. Knowing Jesus, we realize God is not an angry tyrant ready to ruin us for some offense. Jesus also shows us God isn't some distant, impersonal force untouched by our pain and grief. There are times when the loss of a loved one isolates us in a dark room of grief and anger. In Jesus, we see a God who steps into our hurt and weeps with us.

Jesus did so much more than sympathize with Martha and Mary that day. In the tender, teachable moment, he revealed a truth that must have stunned them and everyone there. Every jaw must have dropped when Jesus stood at their brother's grave and announced, "I am the resurrection and the life. The one who believes in me will live, even though they die; and whoever lives by believing in me will never die" (11:25–26).

Jesus looked at Martha and asked her, "Do you believe this?" (v. 26).

This was the same Martha who had held her brother's hand as his breathing became labored, then irregular and shallow, until finally he was gone. The same Martha who stood composed as her brother's lifeless body was laid in a tomb and sealed four days ago.

Martha said, "Yes, Lord, . . . I believe that you are the Messiah, the Son of God, who is to come into the world" (v. 27).

Under the circumstances, it was an extraordinary statement

of faith. Consider she said this even though her brother had been in the tomb four days. What do *you* say in answer to Jesus's question, "Do you believe this?"

You may be thinking, *Why should I believe someone who makes such an outrageous statement?*

What if the One who made that bold claim told the men to roll the stone away from the opening of the tomb where Lazarus was buried? He's got your attention now. And what if he called Lazarus to come out of the grave? Every head turned and every eye focused on the entrance to the tomb. And what if the man who had been dead four days came walking out alive? Would you believe in him then?

Our eyewitness told us the people who were there mourning at the tomb that day and saw Lazarus walk out alive put their trust in Jesus (v. 45). And little did they know, Jesus was just getting warmed up.

AN EVEN GREATER MIRACLE

When he raised Lazarus from a tomb less than two miles from Jerusalem and announced, "I am the resurrection and the life," Jesus attracted many new followers. It also created a buzz in Jerusalem that fueled an exuberant public display when he entered the city riding on a donkey, just as the prophet Zechariah said the Messiah would do (John 12:9–15; Zechariah 9:9). Because people were waving palm branches to celebrate his arrival, that day would come to be known as Palm Sunday.

Raising Lazarus did something else. It set in motion events that would lead to Jesus's execution at the hands of Roman soldiers, who were experts in crucifixion. By nine o'clock Friday morning, just five days after his triumphal entry into Jerusalem, they had scourged Jesus almost to the point of death, paraded his brutalized body through the streets of the city to the site of his execution, and there, with his grieving mother watching, nailed him to a cross along with two thieves.

Shortly after three, a soldier ran his spear into Jesus's side to confirm his death. He got the evidence he was looking for, and Jesus was pronounced dead after six hours on the cross. His body would be taken down from the cross and wrapped in a shroud with seventy-five pounds of myrrh supplied by another one of those fascinating characters who came into Jesus's life. His name was Nicodemus.

Nicodemus was the high-ranking Pharisee who had ventured to meet with Jesus under the cover of darkness (John 3:1–21). His colleagues had rejected Jesus, but he had to see for himself and decide. That night, Nicodemus took the first step in his journey to faith in Jesus. That night, he heard the greatest news ever announced. The good news that continues to captivate the hearts of millions today just as it has through the centuries, ever since Jesus first shared it with a man who came to him with questions: "For God so loved the world that he gave his one and only Son, that whoever believes in him shall not perish but have eternal life" (v. 16).

Another wealthy and high-ranking religious leader who had become a secret follower of Jesus provided the tomb where Jesus's shrouded body was laid to rest that Friday afternoon. The tomb was sealed and guarded by a Roman soldier to prevent any mischief. That Friday night and Saturday everyone thought the remarkable but tragic story of Jesus was over.

But early Sunday morning, just as the day was dawning, Peter and John listened to Mary Magdalene's incredible tale. She had already been to the tomb, and things were amiss. The tomb that had been sealed and guarded was open—and the body was gone (20:1–2)! They set out running for the tomb to see for themselves. John was younger and faster and arrived at the tomb first. He bent and looked in. He was astonished and bewildered by what he saw. Peter was older and bolder. When he finally made it to the tomb, he went right in—breathless from the run, I suspect.

John described the scene for us. After Peter arrived, he followed him into the tomb, focusing his attention on the shelf where Jesus's body was laid Friday afternoon.

This was very strange indeed! If someone had removed the body, surely they would have taken it wrapped in the shroud. Yet here was the shroud and the face cloth. They were there, but the body was gone. The face cloth was not lying with the shroud but "folded up in a place by itself" (v. 7 ESV). What grave robber would take the time to fold the face cloth? For John the evidence was clear and offered only one reasonable conclusion. Jesus had risen from the dead! John told us in that moment "he saw and believed" (v. 8).

THOMAS'S MOMENT

There was a moment in his life when my friend Tom saw and believed. He and Dina were living in California. Faith wasn't part of their relationship. One morning Dina awoke with the idea she wanted to return to Jesus.

"Do what you need to do," Tom told her, but he stayed home when she left for church. With his engineering background, Tom had not seen or heard evidence that was convincing to him. But there came a day when, like John, Tom looked at the evidence and put his trust in Jesus, and he never turned back. It's interesting that Tom's namesake among Jesus's band of disciples was a man who was also a holdout when it came to believing without seeing the evidence for himself.

Thomas, the fearless disciple who, knowing the risk, had been ready to go to Bethany near Jerusalem and die with Jesus (John 11:16), was unmoved by the reports that others had seen Jesus alive. He said so in no uncertain terms: "Unless I see the nail marks in his hands . . . I will not believe" (20:25).

The Sunday following Easter, Jesus appeared again in the house where the disciples were gathered. Thomas was with them this time. Jesus invited Thomas to touch him and see his hands. "Stop doubting and believe," he said to Thomas (v. 27).

In that moment, Thomas's doubt gave way to confident faith. "My Lord and my God!" he proclaimed in awe of the risen Christ standing before him (v. 28). His bold confession of faith provided John the grand finale for his gospel. It's the truth John had wanted us to see since the first word of the book. John told us plainly why he wrote his gospel: "These are written that you may believe that Jesus is the Messiah, the Son of God, and that by believing you may have life in his name" (v. 31).

We can say what we want about what happened in Jerusalem in the spring of AD 33, but the eyewitnesses (and there were hundreds) who saw Jesus alive after his crucifixion were convinced he rose from the dead. Their confidence in his resurrection transformed their lives. The crucifixion of Jesus was a crushing blow that left them sad and fearful. Now they were bold and joyful. Having seen Jesus risen from the dead, they fearlessly spread the stunning news around the world. Some suffered a martyr's death rather than deny what they knew to be true: Jesus rose from the dead.

Hours before the trauma of the cross, Jesus prepared his friends for his departure. "You believe in God," he told them in John 14:1. It was a statement of fact. No doubt, 100 percent of the people in the room when Jesus spoke these words believed in God.

Jesus's words were not just for those in the room. They are also his invitation to you and me. "You believe in God," he said. "Believe also in me" (v. 1).

That same night, knowing they were facing difficult days, Jesus gave his friends a glimpse of the hope awaiting them. His words were spoken to fortify them (and us in our grief). "Do not let your hearts be troubled," he encouraged them. "My Father's house has many rooms, and I'm going there to prepare a place for you. One day I'll come back and take you to be with me so that you may be there in the Father's house with me" (vv. 1–3, author's paraphrase). There is our hope.

BRIGHT HOPE ON A DARK DAY

I'm thinking again of my friend Tom. When I got a call that Tom had died, I went to be with Dina and their four grown children.

Just like Lazarus's sisters, Mary and Martha, Tom's two sisters were also there. We gathered around the hospital bed in the living room, where Tom lay shrouded under a white sheet. I told this dear grieving family how Jesus had cried with Lazarus's sisters and how he also cared deeply for them. I repeated Jesus's words spoken at the graveside of his friend: Whoever "believes in me will live, even though they die" (John 11:25).

As a gentle rain fell from dark, heavy clouds that morning, we shed our tears together. We grieved because Tom was not with us. We grieved because his story didn't end the way we had prayed it would. But here's what you need to know: We were not without hope. This was not the end of Tom's story.

Billy Graham adapted the words of Dwight L. Moody, another man renowned for his proclamation of the good news of Jesus: "Someday you'll read or hear that Billy Graham is dead. Don't you believe a word of it! I will be more alive than I am now. I will just have changed my address. I will have gone into the presence of God."[1]

How could Billy be so sure? Some may say Billy Graham was a great man who preached the gospel to more people than anyone else in history. Others may say he was a good man who loved his wife, Ruth, and lived a life of great integrity. Some will point out that world leaders called on him for his wisdom.

Well, it's good to tell others about Jesus. It's admirable to love your wife and live with integrity. It's rare to be asked to advise heads of state. But none of that was the source of Billy Graham's confidence.

So how could he be so sure? Likewise, how could Dina and Tom's children be so confident Tom's story isn't over? Quite honestly, I've written each page of this book with this moment in mind. Let me ask you: Would you like to live with that same confidence? Would you like to be sure on the day that will come for every one of us that a place is prepared in heaven for you? With all my heart, dear reader, that confident hope of a home in heaven and a life of joy and purpose here and now is what I want for you.

Standing at the graveside of his friend, Jesus told us how all this is possible: "The one who believes in me will live, even though they die" (John 11:25). His invitation still stands, by the way. "You believe in God; *believe also in me*" (14:1).

The greatest evidence that God is for you is this: He sent his Son to live a sinless life, die a vicarious death, and rise from the grave victorious so that you and I could live free from the fear of death. Yes, death separates us from ones we love, but not forever! The apostle Paul said it like this:

> When the perishable has been clothed with the imperishable, and the mortal with immortality, then the saying that is written will come true: "Death has been swallowed up in victory."
>
> "Where, O death, is your victory?
> Where, O death, is your sting?"
>
> . . . Thanks be to God! He gives us the victory through our Lord Jesus Christ.
>
> Therefore, my dear brothers and sisters, stand firm. Let nothing move you. Always give yourselves fully to the work of the Lord, because you know that your labor in the Lord is not in vain. (1 Corinthians 15:54–55, 57–58)

In life and in death, you can be sure God is for you because . . .

God sent his Son so you can live forgiven, free, and forever.

PRAYER

Lord Jesus, I believe you died on the cross for my sins. I believe you were buried and rose again on the third day. Your resurrection from the dead is all the proof I need that you are who you say you are and that your promises are true. I am trusting in you, Lord Jesus. I believe your promise that death will not be the end of my story. When my journey here is complete, take me to live forever in the place you have prepared for me. In your name I pray. Amen.

TALK IT OVER

1. What evidence do we have for the resurrection of Jesus?

2. Jesus made a promise that if we believe in him, we will live even though we die. If it's true that he rose from the dead, what does that tell us about the claims and promises he made?

3. If you haven't done so already, is there any reason why you can't put your trust in Jesus today? Will you take a moment and make the words of the prayer at the end of this chapter your own prayer to God? If you did that, take a moment to write today's date and sign your name on the lines below as a reminder of the decision you made today. Then I encourage you to tell someone about your decision to trust Jesus.

Today I decided to trust in Jesus.

Signed: ______________________________

Date: ______________________________

A SONG TO LIFT YOUR SPIRIT

"Our God" by Chris Tomlin

Chapter 11

YOUR BEST LIFE

A spiritual gift is given to each of us so we can help each other.

1 Corinthians 12:7 NLT

Do nothing from selfish ambition or conceit, but in humility count others more significant than yourselves. Let each of you look not only to his own interests, but also to the interests of others.

Philippians 2:3–4 ESV

The airmen of Joint Task Force-Bravo (JTF-Bravo) are engaged in a high-stakes mission to save thousands of American lives. Along with their other responsibilities, they're working day and night to disrupt the flow of deadly illegal drugs into the United States. Chief Master Sergeant Geoffrey Preudhomme and I traveled to Soto Cano Air Base—about fifty miles northwest of Tegucigalpa, the capital city of Honduras—to visit these heroes while I was assigned as the command chaplain for Air Combat Command.

We had a team of chaplains and chaplain assistants on site with an equally vital mission—to ensure the airmen at Soto Cano could practice their faith even when they were far from home. They were busy leading worship services, teaching Bible studies, and facilitating layperson-led religious services for groups in which a chaplain of that faith community wasn't available.

The chaplain team at JTF-Bravo were there to care for their fellow airmen in other ways as well. Chaplains work well with community resources from medical staff, social workers, civilian clergy, first sergeants, and others to provide an integrated approach to prevention and care. In more than thirty years of active-duty service, I've never met a commander, regardless of religious affiliation, who didn't place a high value on the care chaplains and chaplain assistants provide for their airmen. For one thing, they solve a lot of problems before they can show up on the commander's desk. Military leaders see the difference chaplains make for the airmen under their command. Ask any commander, and he or she will always tell you they want their chaplain teams spending more time in the workplaces with airmen. They want them there building relationships so that when airmen find themselves in crises, they have trusted friends they can call, people they can talk to confidentially. They know this saves lives and helps airmen stay focused on the mission.

This is especially true for those who are deployed. Being away from home doesn't mean the drama of life goes on hold. In fact, it seems to be the perfect opportunity for life to throw its most intense drama at us. As soon as a military member gets deployed, that's when their teenager wrecks the car, or they get a message from the Red Cross about a death in the family, or a Dear John email arrives from a significant other, ending the relationship. It's when more than a few military men have found out their marriages were over. I remember a time we chaplains formed a

Dear John support group for them. Deployments have always been tough on families.

Business travel and heavy workloads can have the same effect on families in the civilian workforce. I'm convinced chaplain care is as beneficial to civilian employees and company leaders as it is for military members and their leaders. Company decision-makers would be wise to consider the benefits of chaplain care and discover what military leaders have always known.

THE CHAPEL HIKE

Part of our reason for traveling to JTF-Bravo was to see firsthand the work its chaplain team was doing to take care of airmen. We were also going to cheer the chaplains on, see if someone needed help, and encourage them. You could say we were going there to be chaplains to the chaplains and their chaplain assistants.[1] When we were planning the trip, someone from JTF-Bravo invited Chief Preudhomme and me to join them on their monthly chapel hike, which happened to be scheduled for the time we would be there. I said, "Sure, sign us up." I thought, *How tough could a chapel hike be?*

"It'll be fun," they said.

It turns out the innocuous-sounding chapel hike to a remote village would involve climbing up the steep, unrelenting incline of a rocky, barefaced mountain under a blazing sun on a cloudless day. In addition, each of us would be carrying a backpack loaded with forty pounds of food, plus our water and snacks. If I had known then what I know now, I would have had two words for the chapel team who invited us to help carry supplies to this village: Amazon Prime.

There must have been between fifty and sixty airmen who made the trek up the mountain that day, each carrying a load of rice, flour, oil, and beans to folks who needed more than a "God bless you" from us to feed their families.

Would you believe me if I told you all that food was purchased with money given by these young Americans, out of their own pockets? It's true. After buying the supplies, these same airmen volunteered their off-duty time to divide the food into backpacks for the hike. They did this once every month, giving their money and volunteering their time for projects like this to make a difference in the communities outside JTF-Bravo. This kind of thing happens wherever American military men and women are stationed around the world.

Early in the morning on the day of the hike, we all met outside the chapel and picked up our backpacks. After a few words from a chaplain, we bowed our heads, and someone prayed. We loaded up on a couple of buses that carried us and our ton of food supplies to the drop-off point at the edge of a small village. Without a lot of chatter, we unloaded the buses and hoisted our backpacks with the precious cargo onto our backs. Our leaders stepped out at what seemed like an ambitious pace. Through the morning, we made our way up the steep, unpaved mountain road. The group that started out in a fairly tight cluster became a long serpentine string of hikers, stretching almost a quarter mile in length, making its way slowly up the incline.

I witnessed something beautiful as we climbed. I saw people helping one another. Stronger ones came alongside the struggling ones with an encouraging word, and they'd keep going. Have you discovered how we're stronger when someone is beside us? People shared snacks and a helping hand to pull someone up after a rest. You could see friendships being forged as we climbed the hill. We were in this together.

Several times when the road made a hairpin curve, I noticed an energetic Chief Preudhomme, my battle buddy, up front leading the way, seeming to enjoy the hike with a tight little band of aerobically fit athletes. While I, on the other hand, significantly older than the chief, had a marvelous ministry of presence with the group gasping for air back at the tail end of the snake. It was tough, but we all made it up the hill because we were motivated by a great mission we believed in, and we were there for each other. It was worth the effort. It must have been early afternoon when we reached a small cinder-block school shaded by a little grove of trees, where we found a crowd of men, women, and excited children—who had walked from miles around—waiting for us.

We organized and started handing out the bags of food. Just as we finished, we heard a strange tinkling sound. As we listened, it seemed to be getting louder. I walked to the road and looked back down the hill we had just climbed. In a moment something rounded the curve in the distance. The sound was coming from the roughest-looking ice-cream truck I have ever seen. Bouncing over the rocks exposed in the dirt road, it was straining up the incline, playing "Pop Goes the Weasel." It was the most unlikely scene you can imagine. But for the guy driving the ice-cream truck, it was his lucky day. The kids came running and gathered around. We bought everything he had. We cleaned him out. Every kid there wore a big smile and had an ice-cream cone in each hand. It was a grace-filled moment I'll always treasure.

This story still makes my eyes leak. Back home one day, I realized how that scene was a beautiful illustration of a good life. It was a picture of the life God had given me. The uphill climb. Friends coming alongside with encouragement during the hard times. A worthy mission. Joyful surprises and unexpected grace. And definitely, the ice-cream cones in both hands! I saw it was the perfect image of life at its best.

> **It was a picture of the life God had given me. The uphill climb. Friends coming alongside during the hard times. A worthy mission. Joyful surprises and unexpected grace.**

The Lord has been so good to me through the years. I've been blessed beyond measure by the love and support of a strong and wise wife; daughters, sons-in-law, and grandchildren to make any man proud; faithful and hardworking parents and grandparents;

and family and friends who've made my life wonderful. On top of all that, I know we enjoy this life of freedom and opportunity thanks to the sacrifices of people we'll never know.

As I think back to that climb, I also see how that day on the mountain in Honduras brings to light some of the best nuggets of wisdom handed down to me by heroes I've been privileged to know. I'll close with just three of those nuggets.

LIFE IS BEST WHEN YOU LIVE IT FOR OTHERS

Chase happiness for yourself and you're likely to miss it. Instead, look around and see where you can bring some joy into someone else's life. Start at home. What can you do for the people under the same roof with you? Sit on the floor and play with a toddler. Find a project to do with your teenager. Surprise your spouse. Is there a homebound senior in your family or in your community? Go visit and take them a peach milkshake. Send a happy card and enclose a photo of your family. Get to know your neighbors. Enjoy a conversation over the fence. Share some fruit from your tree or cookies from your oven. Remember a child's birthday with a small gift. Flash a smile and say a greeting to a stranger you pass in the neighborhood. It will lift their day and yours too. There are churches and charities across our country doing heroic things for others. Find one and jump in. They're delivering meals to seniors. They're tutoring and mentoring students. They're packaging meals for hungry kids. They're serving in prison ministries. They're rescuing women from traffickers. You can volunteer. Can't volunteer? You can give. Can't give? You can pray. Your serving, giving, and praying might take you to the other side of the tracks or the other side of the world, where you could be the answer to somebody's prayers.

There are two large bodies of water in Israel. One is the Sea of Galilee. Streams of water pour into the Sea of Galilee, and the Jordan River flows out the south end. The Sea of Galilee teems with abundant life. In contrast, water flows from the Jordan River into the Dead Sea and stays. Water doesn't flow out of the Dead Sea. It's one of the saltiest bodies of water on the planet.[2] The result is . . . well, they call it the Dead Sea.

I think you get my point. Life can't flourish where you're only a consumer of the grace and goodness that flows from God and others *to you*. But when the grace and blessings you receive flow *through you*, it's life-giving for you and others. "Through you" makes for a better life than just "to you." In your search for hope, you'll probably start out on the road To You. That's the right place to begin the journey. You'll need God's help and the help of others too. But then, when you come to the road marked Through You, I recommend you take it. That's the road that leads you to enduring hope. Stay on it and you'll also discover significance and joy.

Jesus said,

> "I was hungry and you gave me something to eat, I was thirsty and you gave me something to drink, I was a stranger and you invited me in. . . ."
>
> . . . "Lord, when did we see you hungry . . . or thirsty . . . ? When did we see you a stranger? . . ."
>
> The King will reply, "Truly I tell you, whatever you did for one of the least of these . . . , you did it for me." (Matthew 25:35, 37–38, 40)

I wonder if you'll see someone this week just holding on in quiet desperation. They can see no light in their darkness. What would happen if they knew someone sees them? Imagine if someone was willing to step into their hurt or sit with them for a while and listen. I wonder if some small expression of kindness could be the infusion of hope they need. Even if it doesn't change their situation, the encouragement could give them the strength to press on. Could your good deed help them see God's love in a way they've never seen it before? Jesus said it like this: "Let your light shine before others, that they may see your good deeds and glorify your Father in heaven" (Matthew 5:16).

Someone has said the first forty years of a person's life are about achieving success and the next forty years are about finding significance. I have to admit there have been times I was tempted to believe significance comes with a title. More than a few have bought into the myth that the greater your net worth, the greater your significance. Jesus turned all that on its head. It was Matthew, the tax-collecting thief turned Christ follower, who recorded a Jesus truth so radical it must have sounded crazy to the people who first heard it, or at best like a well-intentioned bit of idealistic misinformation. It still sounds a little crazy in our culture today.

> Jesus called them together and said, "You know that the rulers of the Gentiles lord it over them, and their high officials exercise authority over them. Not so with you. Instead, whoever wants to become great among you must be your servant, and whoever wants to be first must be your slave—just as the Son of Man did not come to be served, but to serve, and to give his life as a ransom for many." (Matthew 20:25–28)

Jesus just gave us his mission statement. Did you catch it? He came to serve and give his life so others could live. Hours before he was crucified, Jesus acted out that mission statement for his astonished friends. Once again John was the eyewitness who captured it for us. It was the tenderest, most profound demonstration of humility the world has ever seen. Who could have imagined God on his knees washing dirty feet? What could bring almighty God, the Maker of heaven and earth, to his knees? Only love. Not just any love, but a love unlike anything they'd ever known. Put yourself in that upper room in Jerusalem, lit by flickering oil lamps, as the Son of God rose from the low table where the bread and wine were waiting. He had everyone's attention. What was this he was doing?

> Jesus knew that the Father had put all things under his power, and that he had come from God and was returning to God; so he got up from the meal, took off his outer clothing, and wrapped a towel around his waist. After that, he poured water into a basin and began to wash his disciples' feet, drying them with the towel that was wrapped around him. . . .
>
> When he had finished washing their feet, he put on his clothes. . . . "Do you understand what I have done for you?" he asked them. "You call me 'Teacher' and 'Lord,' and rightly so, for that is what I am. Now that I, your Lord and Teacher, have washed your feet, you also should wash one another's feet. I have set you an example that you should do as I have done for you." (John 13:3–5, 12–15)

Why did Jesus wash their feet? He was showing them and us something profound. Don't miss it! The Creator, the Maker of heaven and earth, laid aside the regal robe of the privileges that were rightfully his as God, and he put on our uniform. The uniform he put on identified him as the lowest rank among us. Almighty God put on our frail humanity and wrapped the towel of a servant around his waist (Philippians 2:5–8).

Don't think Jesus washed his disciples' feet in the final hours before his death because he was so concerned about them having dirty feet. So what was he concerned about, and what was he saying to them that night?

As he washed their feet, Jesus was showing them the meaning of his life and death. He wanted his friends to understand he had come as the servant who would suffer rejection, abuse, and death for them, just as the prophet Isaiah said the Messiah would do (Isaiah 53). His sacrifice would be for their cleansing. And there is more. He was also giving them an example to follow. In the past, they had argued over who was the greatest among them (Mark 9:30–37). From now on they were to serve one another and others.

Here's how the apostle Paul saw it: He was concerned about Jesus followers who might be so nearsighted they have trouble seeing beyond themselves. From a Roman prison where he was being held because of his faith in Jesus, he wrote this prescription that still helps us get our lives in focus: "Do nothing out of selfish ambition or vain conceit. Rather, in humility value others above yourselves, not looking to your own interests but each of you to the interests of the others" (Philippians 2:3–4).

I should clarify something at this point. I don't want to be misunderstood. I'm not talking about making sure my good deeds outweigh my bad deeds so that one day when I stand before God, I can point to all the good stuff I've done for others. If being good were the way to heaven, then why was it necessary for God to send a Savior to sacrifice his life in our place? And how good is good enough? You could never be sure. That would be a terrible way to live and a terrible way to die, always trying to be good enough and never sure whether you did enough to measure up.

But here's the good news: Being right with God is not about doing good works, not even religious works. Paul's letter to the believers in Ephesus helps us understand this. "It is by grace you have been saved, through faith—and this is not from yourselves, it is the gift of God—not by works, so that no one can boast. For we are God's handiwork, created in Christ Jesus to do good works, which God prepared in advance for us to do" (Ephesians 2:8–10).

Look at that beautiful word *grace*. Not in response to anything you've ever done or ever will do, but out of the infinite reservoir of his loving-kindness, God offers you a gift. That gift is a life free from guilt and fear. It's a life of purpose and the power to change. It's a life that doesn't end with the grave. That gift is in his Son, Jesus. That gift is free to all who receive Jesus. Yes, there are good works for us to do, but let's make sure we get the order right. We don't do good to win points with God and get something from him, whether it's his help in this life or it's heaven in the life to come. We want to do good because God has already given us life's greatest gift when he gave us his Son.

When we receive God's Son, something happens in the way we see the world. We begin to see beyond ourselves and focus on the needs and interests of others. With a focus like that, I believe we can change the world—for somebody! When we show up on someone's worst day, they just might see a path to hope they didn't see before.

A ONE-WORD SERMON

William's father died when he was just fourteen years old. He worked as an apprentice to a pawnbroker to earn a little income for his family. He came to know and hate poverty at a young age. When he became a follower of Christ at age fifteen, he wrote in his diary, "God shall have all there is of William Booth."[3]

In 1878 William and his wife, Catherine, rebranded their mission, where they had been serving the poor of East London since 1865. They gave their mission a name that is respected around the world for the good work they do: the Salvation Army. William Booth once said, "While women weep, as they do now, I'll fight; while little children go hungry, I'll fight; while men go to prison, in and out, in and out, as they do now, I'll fight—while there is a drunkard left, while there is a poor lost girl upon the streets, where there remains one dark soul without the light of God—I'll fight! I'll fight to the very end!"[4]

Near the end of his life, having lost his eyesight and with his health failing, William sent a telegram to inspire and give direction to his Salvation Army officers after he was gone. Some say he sent it to be read to the last annual meeting of the Salvation Army before his death on August 20, 1912. Some say it was a final Christmas message he sent out to his officers serving in more than fifty countries around the world. What's so remarkable about the message? It had only one word!

Imagine summing up your life and work in a single word. Imagine setting the course of a global organization for the next century with one word. Jesus did something like that when he put a towel around his waist, bent to his knees, and washed his disciples' feet. He summed up his life and ministry in one simple act. And he gave us our direction for the rest of our lives. William Booth did the same thing in his one-word telegram.

It was about a hundred years after Booth sent that single word that I ran into two Salvation Army officers in line ahead of me to board a plane. They were a husband-and-wife team, partners in ministry like William and Catherine Booth. I knew the story of the one-word message. I couldn't resist. I struck up a conversation, recalling the story, and asked them, "So do you know what the word was?"

I was blown away. A century after it was sent, this couple knew the word! In fact, they were on a mission that very day that was faithful to that one-word vector they received from William Booth a century before. The word was *others*.[5]

I'm grateful God was kind enough to see a rudderless nineteen-year-old sitting in a music practice room at LSU and send him on a mission to serve God by serving others. For Ruth and me, life's greatest adventure has been discovering, in each new assignment and in each new season, who those others are. I wouldn't trade our journey for anything in the world.

For career military men and women, retirement can be disorienting. You leave your house, your friends, your church, your doctor, and your mission. You hang up the uniform and search for a new identity and a new mission. Before we left Washington, DC, God directed my attention to a Scripture verse. It became my vector, my continuing mission for this season of my life. This passage reminds me to keep the focus on others: "My only aim is to finish the race and complete the task the Lord Jesus has given me—the task of testifying to the good news of God's grace" (Acts 20:24).

LIFE IS BEST WHEN YOU LIVE IT WITH OTHERS

Whether it's with a spouse, family, friend, small group, team, neighbor, life is always better together. Joy is doubled when you share it with someone. Maybe that's why most people don't go sightseeing alone. Families come together to celebrate a new baby, someone's new job, or a milestone birthday. Recently, while four generations of our family were together, we celebrated a twelve-year-old niece's report card. She had all A's and a bright face. That's what families do. In our family there's a continuous conversation throughout any given day on a three-generation text thread seasoned with plenty of pictures and emojis. That may be more family togetherness than you're looking for, but we're having a blast with it.

> **Joy is doubled when you share it with someone.**

I love the way military people create extended families wherever they go, especially at overseas bases. We celebrated holidays, birthdays, and promotions together. We became aunts or uncles to one another's kids. I remember that when friends left Yokota Air Base, heading to another assignment, a crowd of chapel-goers would gather at the terminal to see them off. With all the hilarity, hugs, and tears, you'd think these folks had known one another all their lives. For us it was like a member of the family was leaving home. And it was! Here's what military people know that may be helpful to you right now, right where you are. A great assignment (or a great job) is not about the location. It's about the people around you. In fact, sometimes the assignment you didn't want often turns out to be your favorite, not because it was where you wanted to be but because you reached out and made friends who became your family there.

That was certainly true for my wife's parents. They didn't ask for an assignment to Incirlik Air Base, Turkey. It was probably the *last* place they wanted to go. It was too far from their beloved home state of South Carolina and their aging parents. It also meant they'd have to leave the assignment they had asked for again and again every three years: Charleston, South Carolina. Charleston was where they'd always wanted to be, and they loved being there. Along with all that, Incirlik promised to be a difficult assignment because of tensions between our two countries at the time. It turned out to be just as difficult as forecast. Yet during those two years in Turkey they made the closest friendships of all their years in the Air Force.

After retirement, their group of friends vacationed together each fall for decades. Every year, a different couple in the "Turkey Group" planned the trip. As the years rolled on, one by one they succumbed to health issues that impacted their annual gatherings. In September 2001, the group adjusted their plans and gathered in Springfield, Missouri, to rally around their dear friend John as his wife, Evelyn, ended her long battle with cancer. While they were together, they watched in horror as terrorists flew passenger planes into the World Trade Center towers. Through all the heartache and trauma of that week, they found strength and comfort in being together. As the years passed, there would be so many more happy times together before they would lose Pasco and then Doris. One by one the others became too frail to travel. Through it all they continued to love and support one another. That's what families do.

Sometimes life is an uphill climb. God never intended for you to climb alone. Through the pandemic, multiple historic floods, fires, and freezes, and economic challenges, the past several years have been difficult. How many times have we heard the word *unprecedented*? I've seen more anxiety and heartbreak than I've ever seen before. For many, these have been times of crushing sorrow. These times have also revealed the heroes among us. I've witnessed extraordinary acts of kindness and generosity. And I've experienced the truth more powerfully than ever that being connected with others in a caring community saves lives and offers hope when life is hard.

In recent months, I saw a small group in our church rally around one of their members through the illness and death of his wife. I saw someone generously help a young family in despair after losing their income. I've seen folks taking care of their elderly neighbors during a freeze. I've seen a man with a boat and a buddy out rescuing neighbors during an epic flood. Time and again I've seen ordinary folks do extraordinary things because they were willing to see someone's need and step into their hurt. They came alongside someone at just the right time with a comforting presence, an encouraging word, a prayer, and the help needed. Sometimes that perfect timing came from a tip that got the right care to the right person at the right time. Forgive my Air Force lingo, but that looks like precision-guided care to me. That's how God works! Here's what I know to be true: There are just a few things essential to life, and hope is one of them. Finding hope has always been a team sport, and God seems to delight in putting the team together. You need a team. And somewhere, I suspect there's a team that needs you.

LIFE IS BEST WHEN YOU LIVE IT WITH GRATITUDE

The difference is amazing when you look around you and see what a gift you've been given. I know, beyond a doubt, that grateful people live better lives. They probably live longer lives too. Not only does gratitude make your life better, but I can say for sure that when you live with a grateful heart, life is better for the people around you.

Years ago I was on a long transatlantic flight. I noticed the man on my left bowed his head and silently gave thanks for his meal. He smiled and expressed his thanks to the flight attendant when she picked up his tray. Later he opened a pocket-size, very worn New Testament. Its loose pages were held together by a thick rubber band he slipped off the book before he spent some time reading from it. He could not have been more pleasant to those around him. It seemed he had a great flight and enjoyed the trip.

The fellow directly across the aisle on my right was angry the entire trip. He was upset about the meal. He complained about the seat back. He was not happy about the temperature. Nothing could please him. He (and the flight attendant trying to help him) had a miserable trip. Just look at that, two men on the same flight, sitting a few feet from each other, breathing the same air, eating the same meal, making the same trip—yet the difference in their experiences could hardly be greater. I've never forgotten the contrast.

Wherever you're headed on your journey, whatever your circumstance, I believe if you open your heart to God's grace, you'll see something beautiful. You'll see a past with all its regrets and shame wiped clean. You'll see you're not alone in your sorrow, your struggle, or your pain. You'll see the hope of a brighter day awaiting you. You'll see that God is for you. And there's more! You will see how loved you are and catch a glimpse of your infinite worth. You'll see a mission with your name on it and a purpose for your life. You just may see you're living with an ice-cream cone in both hands!

SONGS TO LIFT YOUR SPIRIT

"Grateful" by Elevation Worship

"Be Alright" by Evan Craft, Danny Gokey, and Redimi2

TEN REASONS YOU CAN BE SURE GOD IS STILL FOR YOU

1. God is always watching over you.
2. God has been good to you in the past.
3. God has prepared someone who can provide the encouragement and help you need.
4. God is with you in your darkest hour.
5. Your heavenly Father sees you, and you are his treasure.
6. Jesus invites you to follow him.
7. God restores your hope.
8. God doesn't waste your pain but uses it to accomplish good.
9. God gives you the Holy Spirit to guide you to the truth and help you pray.
10. God sent his Son so you can live forgiven, free, and forever.

ACKNOWLEDGMENTS

It's been said when you see a turtle on a fence post, you know he didn't get there on his own. Having read this book, you can be sure I didn't get here on my own either. Without my best friend and partner in life and ministry, this book would never have happened. Ruth Page has been my constant encourager and sounding board. If there's someone who believes in you the way my wife believes in me, you know how greatly blessed I am, and you know how this book came to be.

There were several friends who supported this project from the first moment it took form in my heart. I'm grateful for Tanya and Kent Whitaker, Marci and Neil Brown, Jennifer and Jamey Webster—who read through the manuscript multiple times and gave me helpful advice that made this a much better book. Kent Whitaker has a story of his own that's full of uncommon grace and the stuff of miracles. His stewardship of that tragic story made him a *New York Times* best-selling author with his book *Murder by Family*. He has served as my mentor throughout this process. In fact, he was the person who encouraged me to attend the Christian writers' conference at Mount Hermon, California, to pitch my manuscript to publishers and agents, which started this journey.

Special thanks to the members, pastors, and staff of River Pointe & West End Church, who listened to my stories and encouraged me to put them in writing. I must thank the men at the Texas prison Carol S. Vance Unit, and one in particular. When I first considered writing this book, I wrote a chapter to test the waters. Shortly after that I was invited to speak to the men incarcerated at the prison on a Sunday afternoon during their weekly chapel service. My message that day was adapted from the chapter I had just written. About a hundred men listened attentively and responded to my message with the kind of openness and generosity every preacher dreams of. After the service, one man dressed in all-white prison garb waited in line to tell me something he thought I needed to hear. What he told me stunned me. "You ought to write a book," he said, "and put this message in it." Well, I heard God speak to me through a man with a history covered by the grace of Jesus, just like mine.

A special thanks to our Air Force friends who still love us like family and have made three decades of life, lived in three-year segments all over the world, seem too short. Thank you to each of them who allowed me to share their stories. I can say our lives are richer and my faith is stronger because we walked part of the journey with you.

I'm grateful for each of the extraordinary men and women who took time out of their busy schedules to write an endorsement for this book. Thank you to my amazing literary agent, Karen Neumair of Credo Communications, who believed in me and this project after reading a few chapters. Her faithful advocacy and encouragement to persevere led me to Kregel Publications. Thank you to Catherine DeVries, Kregel's publisher, for taking a chance on a new author. I'm deeply indebted to Kregel's managing editor Rachel Kirsch, and editors Caryn Rivadeneira, Dori Harrell, Sarah Cross, and Emily Irish for applying their gifts to make *God Is Still for You* a book worth reading. Finally, my heartfelt thanks to a personal hero of mine, Dr. Dondi Costin, president of Liberty University, for adding his foreword and generous endorsement to this book.

NOTES

INTRODUCTION: HOPE IN THE DESERT

1. The outer ring of the Pentagon, occupied by senior military officers.

CHAPTER 1: THE GOD WHO NEVER SLEEPS

1. Since 1944, veterans may qualify for government assistance to pay for education or training.
2. Steven Gertz, "How Do We Know 10 of the Disciples Were Martyred?" *Christianity Today*, August 8, 2008, https://www.christianitytoday.com/2008/08/how-do-we-know-10-of-disciples-were-martyred/.
3. Thomas Moore, "Come, Ye Disconsolate," hymn text, 1816, public domain.
4. "Come as You Are," by Den Glover, David Crowder, and Matt Maher, produced by Capitol CMG, released 2014.
5. "Derek Redmond's Emotional Olympic Story—Injury Mid-Race | Barcelona 1992 Olympics," posted October 31, 2011, by Olympics, YouTube, https://www.youtube.com/watch?v=t2G8KVzTwfw. Derek's injury happens around the 20-second mark and Derek's father appears around the 55-second mark.

CHAPTER 2: ROADBLOCKS AND DETOURS

1. *The Expositor's Greek Testament*, ed. W. Robertson Nicoll, vol. 1, *The Synoptic Gospels*, ed. Alexander Balmain Bruce (Dodd, Mead and Company, 1902), 112–13, https://www.google.com/books/edition

/The_Expositor_s_Greek_Testament/G5cRAAAAYAAJ?hl=en&gbpv=0.

2. R. Laird Harris et al., *Theological Wordbook of the Old Testament,* (Moody Press, 1980), 1:305–7.
3. Footnote for Romans 8:28 in *The Holy Bible, New International Version* (Zondervan, 2011), https://www.biblegateway.com/passage/?search=romans%208%3A28&version=NIV.

CHAPTER 3: A BRASS COIN AND SOLID-GOLD TRUTH

1. U.S. Const. amen. I.
2. My remembrance is that General Mark Welsh, chief of staff of the Air Force, said this to a gathering of Chaplain Corps leadership in Washington, DC, circa 2014.
3. For physical training, airmen of all ranks were required to pass an annual fitness test, which included running a one-and-a-half-mile course within a set time, depending on age and gender. In order to score as many points as possible on the timed run, many airmen ran several times each week.

CHAPTER 4: NIGHT VISION GOGGLES

1. James Stewart, "David—Warrior Artist," *Timeline,* Vermont Public Radio, September 9, 2019, www.vpr.org/programs/2019-09-09/timeline-david-warrior-artist.
2. Stewart, "Timeline."
3. Bill Keith, *Days of Anguish, Days of Hope,* 7th ed. (Stonegate Publishing, 2011). Robert Preston Taylor's story is used in *God Is Still for You* with permission from Bill Keith.
4. Robert Taylor probably recalled Psalm 23 in the King James Version. Here, it is in the English Standard Version.
5. Robert B. Sloan Jr., as quoted in "Former Air Force Chaplain Presented War Heroes Award," Baylor University, January 9, 2004, https://news.web.baylor.edu/news/story/2004/former-air-force-chaplain-presented-war-heroes-award.

6. Lorraine Potter, quoting Robert Taylor, "Former Air Force Chaplain Presented War Heroes Award."
7. Robert Preston Taylor, interview by Ronald E. Marcello, November 2, 1974, transcript, University of North Texas Oral History Program, Arlington, TX. Available on Humanities Texas at https://www.humanitiestexas.org/news/articles/interview-robert-preston-taylor-world-war-ii-pow/.
8. Bill Keith, "Fourth of July: POW Chaplain Redeemed His Agonies," *Baptist Press*, July 1, 2011, www.baptistpress.com/resource-library/news/fourth-of-july-pow-chaplain-redeemed-his-agonies/.
9. Charles Spurgeon, "February 19: Full and Running Over," *Spurgeon's Daily Treasures in the Psalms: Selections from the Classic Treasury of David*, ed. Roger Campbell (Kregel, 2013), 120–21.
10. Charles Spurgeon, *Spurgeon's Daily Treasury from the Psalms*, ed. Robert Backhouse (Crossway, 2002), 60.

CHAPTER 5: ALL US SPARROWS

1. Ethel Waters and Charles T. Samuel, *His Eye Is on the Sparrow: An Autobiography* (Da Capo Press, 1992), 15–16.
2. Waters and Samuel, *His Eye Is on the Sparrow*, 1.
3. Waters and Samuel, *His Eye Is on the Sparrow*, 58–61.
4. Claytee D. White, "Ethel Waters (1896–1977)," BlackPast.org, February 11, 2007, www.blackpast.org/african-american-history/waters-ethel-1896-1977/.
5. Civilla D. Martin, "His Eye Is on the Sparrow," hymn text, 1905, public domain.
6. *Britannica*, "Ethel Waters: American Singer and Actress," accessed August 28, 2021, www.britannica.com/biography/Ethel-Waters.
7. "Ethel Waters," Find a Grave, accessed June 23, 2025, https://www.findagrave.com/memorial/2160/ethel-waters.
8. Michael F. Chandler, "From Earthly Rags to Eternal Riches," *Victorville Daily Press*, May 15, 2021, www.vvdailypress.com/story/lifestyle

/faith/2021/05/15/commentary-ethel-waters-earthly-rags-eternal-riches/5087968001/.

9. Ethel Waters, "Ethel Waters—His eye is on the sparrow—1975–," posted June 22, 2025, by Praise Be His, YouTube, 5 min., 50 sec., https://www.youtube.com/watch?v=I1kt0yY1LlM&list=RDI1kt0yY1LlM&start_radio=1.
10. Robert Jamieson et al., *A Commentary Critical, Experimental, and Practical on the Old and New Testaments*, vol. 3, *Job–Isaiah*, ed. A. R. Fausset (Eerdmans, 1948), 376.
11. Manuel Scott Sr. (1926–2001) was a Black preacher twice named one of America's fifteen greatest Black preachers by *Ebony* magazine. This "I Found a Penny" story is recounted from memory. I heard him tell it at a Southwestern Baptist Theological Seminary chapel service circa 1982, while I was a student there.
12. "Journey's 'Don't Stop Believin'' Passes One Billion Streams on Spotify," My Radio Link, February 28, 2021, www.myradiolink.com/2021/02/28/journeys-dont-stop-believin-passes-one-billion-streams-on-spotify.
13. Jonathan Cain's story and the quotes can be found in an article by Lauren Moraski, "Here's the Story Behind 'Don't Stop Believin',' the Song That Keeps on Giving," *HuffPost*, May 2, 2018, www.huffpost.com/entry/journey-dont-stop-believin_n_5ae9b94de4b022f71a03cef1.
14. Civilla Martin's story can be found in an article by Lindsay Terry, "The Story Behind the Song: His Eye Is on the Sparrow," *St. Augustine Record*, October 29, 2015, https://www.staugustine.com/story/lifestyle/faith/2015/10/30/story-behind-song-his-eye-sparrow/16259645007/.
15. C. Michael Hawn, "History of Hymns: 'His Eye Is On the Sparrow,'" Discipleship Ministries, June 25, 2013, www.umcdiscipleship.org/resources/history-of-hymns-his-eye-is-on-the-sparrow.

CHAPTER 6: OUTLIERS AND OUTCASTS

1. Richard P. Thompson, "Fishing in the First Century," *Illustrated Bible Life*, June–August 2015, 4–7, https://www.nph.com/vcmedia/2422/2422892.pdf.
2. Sarah Mann, "Ancient Routes of Israel," BeinHarim Tourism Services,

November 14, 2021, https://www.beinharimtours.com/ancient-routes-of-israel/.

3. Joel Ryan, "Why Would Jesus Call a Zealot to Be His Disciple," Bible Study Tools, September 5, 2024, https://www.biblestudytools.com/bible-study/topical-studies/why-would-jesus-call-a-zealot-to-be-his-disciple.html.
4. "Exploring the Role and Legacy of Simon the Zealot," Bible Stories Hub, February 18, 2025, https://biblestorieshub.com/exploring-the-role-and-legacy-of-simon-the-zealot/.
5. Joe Debeljuh, "The Bible Provides Examples of Discipleship Relationships," *The Disciple Dilemma*, June 9, 2022, https://thedisciplediemma.com/the-bible-provides-examples-of-discipleship-relationships-guest-blog/.
6. "The Heavenly Vision," Helen Howarth Lemmel, 1922, public domain. The hymn is best known by the first line of its refrain, "Turn Your Eyes upon Jesus."

CHAPTER 7: HOPE LIKE WATER

1. Mene Ukueberuwa, "Remember Todd Beamer of United 93: His Heroism on 9/11 Drew from a Lifetime of Faith and Character," *Wall Street Journal*, September 9, 2021, www.wsj.com/articles/flight-93-united-todd-beamer-9-11-september-eleventh-jihadist-terrorist-attack-11631223355.

CHAPTER 9: YOUR NEW BEST FRIEND

1. John, the gospel writer, uses a word (*telos*) that can mean "to the greatest or most extreme way possible" or "to the end." Both meanings fit the context here. *Strong's*, "G5056—telos," Bible Hub, https://biblehub.com/greek/5056.htm.
2. *Encyclopedia of the Bible*, "Paraclete," Bible Gateway, accessed January 12, 2025, https://www.biblegateway.com/resources/encyclopedia-of-the-bible/Paraclete.
3. *The Broadman Bible Commentary*, ed. Clifton J. Allen, vol. 9, *Luke–John*, ed. William E. Hull (Broadman Press, 1970), 341.

CHAPTER 10: THIS CHANGES EVERYTHING

1. Billy Graham, as quoted in Caleb Lindgren, "Someday You'll Read or Hear That Billy Graham Didn't Really Say That," *Christianity Today*, February 21 2018, www.christianitytoday.com/ct/2018/february-web-only/billy-graham-viral-quote-on-death-not-his-d-l-moody.html.

CHAPTER 11: YOUR BEST LIFE

1. Chaplain assistants in the Air Force are enlisted members of the Chaplain Corps. While their duty title has changed to religious affairs airmen, their mission remains the same: to partner with chaplains in providing spiritual care and facilitating the free exercise of religion.
2. Joyce Chepkemoi, "The World's Saltiest Bodies of Water," WorldAtlas, June 7, 2019, https://www.worldatlas.com/articles/the-world-s-most-saline-bodies-of-water.html.
3. William Booth, as quoted in "William Booth: First General of the Salvation Army," *Christianity Today*, August 8, 2008, www.christianitytoday.com/history/people/activists/william-booth.html.
4. Booth, as quoted in "William Booth."
5. This "Others" telegram story can be found on multiple regional Salvation Army websites, including Salvation Army Tucson's "About Us" page, accessed January 11, 2025, https://www.salvationarmytucson.org/about1-ch7r.

ABOUT THE AUTHOR

Bob Page is the chief of chaplains for Marketplace Chaplains—the oldest and largest provider of workplace chaplain care in the world, with twenty-two hundred chaplains serving 1.5 million employees and family members at six thousand locations in all fifty states, Canada, and Puerto Rico.

After beginning his Air Force career as a navigator on a KC-135A aircraft refueling other aircraft in flight, Bob then served twenty-six years as an Air Force chaplain, including eight months of deployment to Saudi Arabia and Iraq. Bob's civilian ministry includes pastorates in Arkansas, North Carolina, and Texas.

In 2012, while serving as a colonel in the Air Force, the United States Senate confirmed his promotion to brigadier general as the twenty-fourth Air Force deputy chief of chaplains. After serving at the Pentagon in that role for three years, Bob and his wife, Ruth, retired to Texas.

He was inducted into the Louisiana State University Alumni Hall of Distinction in 2014 and LSU's Hall of Honor for Distinguished Military Leadership in 2015.

When Hurricane Harvey devastated the Houston area with more than fifty inches of rain in 2017, River Pointe Church asked Bob to join their staff and lead their countywide effort to disburse a million-dollar relief fund and mobilize thousands of volunteers to help their neighbors recover from the historic flood. Then, as the church's Missions and Care pastor for the next five years, he led its eight thousand members to love God and love people locally and globally.

He and Ruth have two married daughters and five grandchildren, who amaze them daily.

By purchasing this book, you are supporting Marketplace Chaplains, the world's first, largest, and fastest-growing workplace chaplaincy organization.

Since 1984, Marketplace Chaplains has provided a personalized and proactive employee-care service. Our chaplain teams are made up of ethnically diverse men and women who speak a combined total of forty-one languages. Currently our chaplains visit over six thousand worksites in North America every week and care for more than 1.5 million employees and family members.

The author's proceeds from God Is Still for You *go to Marketplace Chaplains as they support employees and their families nationwide.*

Learn more at mchapusa.com or scan the QR code